THE DISCARDED IMAGE

To

ROGER LANCELYN GREEN

THE
DISCARDED
IMAGE

AN INTRODUCTION TO
MEDIEVAL AND RENAISSANCE
LITERATURE

BY

C. S. LEWIS

CAMBRIDGE UNIVERSITY PRESS

CAMBRIDGE

LONDON · NEW YORK · MELBOURNE

Published by the Syndics of the Cambridge University Press
The Pitt Building, Trumpington Street, Cambridge CB2 1RP
Bentley House, 200 Euston Road, London NW1 2DB
32 East 57th Street, New York, NY 10022, USA
296 Beaconsfield Parade, Middle Park, Melbourne 3206, Australia

ISBN 0 521 05551 2 hard covers
ISBN 0 521 09450 X paperback

First published 1964
Reprinted 1964, 1967
First paperback edition 1967
Reprinted 1970, 1971, 1974, 1976

First printed in Great Britain at the University Printing House, Cambridge
Reprinted in Malta by Interprint Ltd

CONTENTS

Contents

PREFACE

This book is based on a course of lectures given more than once at Oxford. Some who attended it have expressed a wish that its substance might be given a more permanent form.

I cannot boast that it contains much which a reader could not have found out for himself if, at every hard place in the old books, he had turned to commentators, histories, encyclopaedias, and other such helps. I thought the lectures worth giving and the book worth writing because that method of discovery seemed to me and seems to some others rather unsatisfactory. For one thing, we turn to the helps only when the hard passages are manifestly hard. But there are treacherous passages which will not send us to the notes. They look easy and aren't. Again, frequent researches *ad hoc* sadly impair receptive reading, so that sensitive people may even come to regard scholarship as a baleful thing which is always taking you *out of* the literature itself. My hope was that if a tolerable (though very incomplete) outfit were acquired beforehand and taken along with one, it might lead *in*. To be always looking at the map when there is a fine prospect before you shatters the 'wise passiveness' in which landscape ought to be enjoyed. But to consult a map before we set out has no such ill effect. Indeed it will lead us to many prospects; including some we might never have found by following our noses.

There are, I know, those who prefer not to go beyond the impression, however accidental, which an old work makes on a mind that brings to it a purely modern sensibility and modern conceptions; just as there are travellers who carry their resolute Englishry with them all over the Continent, mix only with other English tourists, enjoy all they see for its 'quaintness', and have no wish to realise what those ways of life, those churches, those vineyards, mean to the natives. They have their reward. I have no quarrel with people who approach the past in that spirit. I hope they will pick none with me. But I was writing for the other sort.

C. S. L.

MAGDALENE COLLEGE
July 1962

CHAPTER I

THE MEDIEVAL SITUATION

The likeness of unlike things
MULCASTER

Medieval man shared many ignorances with the savage, and some of his beliefs may suggest savage parallels to an anthropologist. But he had not usually reached these beliefs by the same route as the savage.

Savage beliefs are thought to be the spontaneous response of a human group to its environment, a response made principally by the imagination. They exemplify what some writers call pre-logical thinking. They are closely bound up with the communal life of the group. What we should describe as political, military, and agricultural operations are not easily distinguished from rituals; ritual and belief beget and support one another. The most characteristically medieval thought does not arise in that way.

Sometimes, when a community is comparatively homogeneous and comparatively undisturbed over a long period, such a system of belief can continue, of course with development, long after material culture has progressed far beyond the level of savagery. It may then begin to turn into something more ethical, more philosophical, even more scientific; but there will be uninterrupted continuity between this and its savage beginnings. Something like this, it would seem, happened in Egypt.[1] That also is unlike the history of medieval thought.

[1] See *Before Philosophy*, J. A. Wilson, etc. (1949).

The peculiarity of the Middle Ages can be shown by two examples.

Some time between 1160 and 1207 an English priest called Laȝamon wrote a poem called the *Brut*.[1] In it (ll. 15,775 *sq.*) he tells us that the air is inhabited by a great many beings, some good and some bad, who will live there till the world ends. The content of this belief is not unlike things we might find in savagery. To people Nature, and especially the less accessible parts of her, with spirits both friendly and hostile, is characteristic of the savage response. But Laȝamon is not writing thus because he shares in any communal and spontaneous response made by the social group he lives in. The real history of the passage is quite different. He takes his account of the aerial daemons from the Norman poet Wace (*c.* 1155). Wace takes it from Geoffrey of Monmouth's *Historia Regum Britanniae* (before 1139). Geoffrey takes it from the second-century *De Deo Socratis* of Apuleius. Apuleius is reproducing the pneumatology of Plato. Plato was modifying, in the interests of ethics and monotheism, the mythology he had received from his ancestors. If you go back through many generations of those ancestors, then at last you may find, or at least conjecture, an age when that mythology was coming into existence in what we suppose to be the savage fashion. But the English poet knew nothing about that. It is further from him than he is from us. He believes in these daemons because he has read about them in a book; just as most of us believe in the Solar System or in the

[1] Ed. F. Madden, 3 vols. (1847).

2

anthropologists' accounts of early man. Savage beliefs tend to be dissipated by literacy and by contact with other cultures; these are the very things which have created Laȝamon's belief.

My second example is perhaps more interesting. In the fourteenth-century *Pèlerinage de l'Homme* by Guillaume Deguileville, Nature (personified), speaking to a character called Grâcedieu, says that the frontier between their respective realms is the orbit of the Moon.[1] It would be easy to suppose that this is the direct offspring of savage mythopoeia, dividing the sky into a higher region peopled with higher spirits and a lower region peopled with lower. The Moon would be a spectacular landmark between them. But in reality the origins of this passage have very little to do with savage, or even with civilised, religion. By calling the superior *numen* Grâcedieu the poet has worked in something of Christianity; but this is merely a 'wash' spread over a canvas that is not Christian but Aristotelian.

Aristotle, being interested both in biology and in astronomy, found himself faced with an obvious contrast. The characteristic of the world we men inhabit is incessant change by birth, growth, procreation, death, and decay. And within that world such experimental methods as had been achieved in his time could discover only an imperfect uniformity. Things happened in the same way not perfectly nor invariably but 'on the whole' or 'for the most part'.[2] But the world studied by astronomy seemed quite different. No *Nova* had yet been

[1] In Lydgate's trans. (E.E.T.S. ed. F. J. Furnivall, 1899), 3415 *sq.*
[2] *De Gen. Animalium*, 778 a; *Polit.* 1255 b.

observed.[1] So far as he could find out, the celestial bodies were permanent; they neither came into existence nor passed away. And the more you studied them, the more perfectly regular their movements seemed to be. Apparently, then, the universe was divided into two regions. The lower region of change and irregularity he called Nature (φύσις). The upper he called Sky (οὐρανός). Thus he can speak of 'Nature and Sky' as two things.[2] But that very changeable phenomenon, the weather, made it clear that the realm of inconstant Nature extended some way above the surface of the Earth. 'Sky' must begin higher up. It seemed reasonable to suppose that regions which differed in every observable respect were also made of different stuff. Nature was made of the four elements, earth, water, fire, and air. Air, then (and with air Nature, and with Nature inconstancy) must end before Sky began. Above the air, in true Sky, was a different substance, which he called *aether*. Thus 'the *aether* encompasses the divine bodies, but immediately below the aethereal and divine nature comes that which is passible, mutable, perishable, and subject to death'.[3] By the word *divine* Aristotle introduces a religious element; and the placing of the important frontier (between Sky and Nature, Aether and Air) at the Moon's orbit is a minor

[1] There is a tradition that Hipparchus (*fl.* 150 B.C.) detected one (see Pliny, *Nat. Hist.* II, xxiv). The great *Nova* in Cassiopeia of Nov. 1572 was a most important event for the history of thought (see F. R. Johnson, *Astronomical Thought in Renaissance England*, Baltimore, 1937, p. 154).

[2] *Metaphys.* 1072 b. Cf. Dante, *Par.* XXVIII, 42.

[3] *De Mundo*, 392ª. Whether this essay is Aristotle's or merely of the Aristotelian school does not matter for my purpose.

4

detail. But the concept of such a frontier seems to arise far more in response to a scientific than to a religious need. This is the ultimate source of the passage in Deguileville.

What both examples illustrate is the overwhelmingly bookish or clerkly character of medieval culture. When we speak of the Middle Ages as the ages of authority we are usually thinking about the authority of the Church. But they were the age not only of her authority, but of authorities. If their culture is regarded as a response to environment, then the elements in that environment to which it responded most vigorously were manuscripts. Every writer, if he possibly can, bases himself on an earlier writer, follows an *auctour*: preferably a Latin one. This is one of the things that differentiate the period almost equally from savagery and from our modern civilisation. In a savage community you absorb your culture, in part unconsciously, from participation in the immemorial pattern of behaviour, and in part by word of mouth, from the old men of the tribe. In our own society most knowledge depends, in the last resort, on observation. But the Middle Ages depended pre-dominantly on books. Though literacy was of course far rarer then than now, reading was in one way a more important ingredient of the total culture.

To this statement a reservation must however be added. The Middle Ages had roots in the 'barbarian' North and West as well as in that Graeco-Roman tradi-tion which reached them principally through books. I have put the word 'barbarian' in inverted commas because it might otherwise mislead. It might suggest a far greater difference in race and arts and natural capacity than really existed even in ancient times between Roman citizens and those who pressed upon the frontiers of the empire. Long before that empire fell, citizenship had ceased to have any connection with race. Throughout its history its Germanic and (still more) its Celtic neighbours, if once conquered or allied, apparently had no reluctance to assimilate, and no difficulty in assimilating, its civilisation. You could put them into togas and set them to learning rhetoric almost at once. They were not in the least like Hottentots dressed up in bowler hats and pretending to be Europeans. The assimilation was real and often permanent. In a few generations they might be producing Roman poets, jurists, generals. They differed from the older members of the Graeco-Roman world no more than these differed from one another in shape of skull, features, complexion, or intelligence.

The contribution of the barbarian (thus understanding the word) to the Middle Ages will be variously assessed according to the point of view from which we study them. So far as law and custom and the general shape of society are concerned, the barbarian elements may be the most important. The same is true, in one particular way, of one particular art in some countries. Nothing about a literature can be more essential than the language it uses. A language has its own personality; implies an outlook, reveals a mental activity, and has a resonance, not quite the same as those of any other. Not only the vocabulary —*heaven* can never mean quite the same as *ciel*—but the very shape of the syntax is *sui generis*. Hence in the

Germanic countries, including England, the debt of the medieval (and modern) literatures to their barbarian origin is all-pervasive. In other countries, where the Celtic languages and those of the Germanic invaders were both almost completely obliterated by Latin, the situation is quite different. In Middle English literature, after every necessary allowance has been made for French and Latin influences, the tone and rhythm and the very 'feel' of every sentence is (in the sense that we are now giving to the word) of barbarian descent. Those who ignore the relation of English to Anglo-Saxon as a 'merely philological fact' irrelevant to the literature betray a shocking insensibility to the very mode in which literature exists.

For the student of culture in a narrower sense—that is, of thought, sentiment, and imagination—the barbarian elements may be less important. Even for him they are doubtless by no means negligible. Fragments of non-classical Paganism survive in Old Norse, Anglo-Saxon, Irish, and Welsh; they are thought by most scholars to underlie a great deal of Arthurian romance. Medieval love-poetry may owe something to barbarian manners. Ballads, till a very late period, may throw up fragments of prehistoric (if it is not perennial) folklore. But we must see these things in proportion. The Old Norse and Celtic texts were, and remained till modern times, utterly unknown outside a very limited area. Changes in language soon made Anglo-Saxon unintelligible even in England. Elements from the old Germanic and the old Celtic world undoubtedly exist in the later vernaculars.

But how hard we have to look for them! For one reference to Wade or Weland we meet fifty to Hector, Aeneas, Alexander, or Caesar. For one probable relic of Celtic religion dug out of a medieval book we meet, clear and emphatic, a score of references to Mars and Venus and Diana. The debt which the love-poets may owe to the barbarians is shadowy and conjectural; their debt to the classics, or even, as now appears, to the Arabians, is much more certain.

It may perhaps be held that the barbarian legacy is not really less, but only less flaunted and more disguised; even that it is all the more potent for being secret. This might be true as regards the romances and ballads. We must therefore ask how far, or rather in what sense, these are characteristically medieval products. They certainly loomed larger in the eighteenth- and nineteenth-century picture of the Middle Ages than in the reality. There was a good reason why they should. Ariosto, Tasso, and Spenser, the lineal descendants of the medieval romancers, continued to be 'polite literature' right down to the age of Hurd and Warton. The taste for that sort of fiction was kept alive all through the 'Metaphysical' and the Augustan Age. Throughout the same period the ballad also, though often in a somewhat degraded form, had kept alive. Children heard it from their nurses; eminent critics sometimes praised it. Thus the medieval 'Revival' of the eighteenth century revived what was not quite dead. It was along this line that we worked back to medieval literature; following to its source a stream which flowed past our door. As a result, Romance and Ballad coloured men's idea of the Middle Ages somewhat excessively. Except among scholars they do so still. Popular iconography—a poster, a joke in *Punch*—wishing to summon up the idea of the Medieval, draws a knight errant with castles, distressed damsels, and dragons *quant. suff.* in the background.

For the popular impression, as often, a defence can be made. There is a sense in which the Romances and Ballads perhaps really deserve to rank as the characteristic or representative product of the Middle Ages. Of the things they have left us these have proved the most widely and permanently pleasurable. And though things which in varying degrees resemble them can be found elsewhere, they are, in their total effect, unique and irreplaceable. But if by calling them characteristic we mean that the sort of imagination they embody was the principal, or even the very frequent, occupation of medieval men, we shall be mistaken. The eerie quality of some ballads and the hard, laconic pathos of others—the mystery, the sense of the illimitable, the elusive reticence of the best romances—these things stand apart from the habitual medieval taste. In some of the greatest medieval literature they are wholly lacking: in the Hymns, in Chaucer, in Villon. Dante can take us through all the regions of the dead without ever once giving us the *frisson* we get from *The Wife of Usher's Well* or The Chapel Perilous. It looks as if the Romances and such Ballads were in the Middle Ages, as they have remained ever since, truancies, refreshments, things that can live only on the margin of the mind, things whose very charm depends on their not being 'of the centre' (a locality which Matthew Arnold possibly overvalued).

At his most characteristic, medieval man was not a dreamer nor a wanderer. He was an organiser, a codifier, a builder of systems. He wanted 'a place for everything and everything in the right place'. Distinction, definition, tabulation were his delight. Though full of turbulent activities, he was equally full of the impulse to formalise them. War was (in intention) formalised by the art of heraldry and the rules of chivalry; sexual passion (in intention), by an elaborate code of love. Highly original and soaring philosophical speculation squeezes itself into a rigid dialectical pattern copied from Aristotle. Studies like Law and Moral Theology, which demand the ordering of very diverse particulars, especially flourish. Every way in which a poet can write (including some in which he had much better not) is classified in the Arts of Rhetoric. There was nothing which medieval people liked better, or did better, than sorting out and tidying up. Of all our modern inventions I suspect that they would most have admired the card index.

This impulse is equally at work in what seem to us their silliest pedantries and in their most sublime achievements. In the latter we see the tranquil, indefatigable, exultant energy of passionately systematic minds bringing huge masses of heterogeneous material into unity. The perfect examples are the *Summa* of Aquinas and Dante's *Divine Comedy*; as unified and ordered as the Parthenon or the *Oedipus Rex*, as crowded and varied as a London terminus on a bank holiday.

But there is a third work which we can, I think, set beside these two. This is the medieval synthesis itself, the whole organisation of their theology, science, and history into a single, complex, harmonious mental Model of the Universe. The building of this Model is conditioned by two factors I have already mentioned: the essentially bookish character of their culture, and their intense love of system.

They are bookish. They are indeed very credulous of books. They find it hard to believe that anything an old *auctour* has said is simply untrue. And they inherit a very heterogeneous collection of books; Judaic, Pagan, Platonic, Aristotelian, Stoical, Primitive Christian, Patristic. Or (by a different classification) chronicles, epic poems, sermons, visions, philosophical treatises, satires. Obviously their *auctours* will contradict one another. They will seem to do so even more often if you ignore the distinction of kinds and take your science impartially from the poets and philosophers; and this the medievals very often did in fact though they would have been well able to point out, in theory, that poets feigned. If, under these conditions, one has also a great reluctance flatly to disbelieve anything in a book, then here there is obviously both an urgent need and a glorious opportunity for sorting out and tidying up. All the apparent contradictions must be harmonised. A Model must be built which will get everything in without a clash; and it can do this only by becoming intricate, by mediating its unity through a great, and finely ordered, multiplicity. This task, I believe, the Medievals would in any case have undertaken.

But they had a further inducement in the fact that it had already been begun, and indeed carried a fair way. In the last age of antiquity many writers—some of them will meet us in a later chapter—were, perhaps half-consciously, gathering together and harmonising views of very different origin: building a syncretistic Model not only out of Platonic, Aristotelian, and Stoical, but out of Pagan and Christian elements. This Model the Middle Ages adopted and perfected.

In speaking of the perfected Model as a work to be set beside the *Summa* and the *Comedy*, I meant that it is capable of giving a similar satisfaction to the mind, and for some of the same reasons. Like them it is vast in scale, but limited and intelligible. Its sublimity is not the sort that depends on anything vague or obscure. It is, as I shall try to show later, a classical rather than a Gothic sublimity. Its contents, however rich and various, are in harmony. We see how everything links up with everything else; at one, not in flat equality, but in a hierarchical ladder. It might be supposed that this beauty of the Model was apparent chiefly to us who, no longer accepting it as true, are free to regard it—or reduced to regarding it—as if it were a work of art. But I believe this is not so. I think there is abundant evidence that it gave profound satisfaction while it was still believed in. I hope to persuade the reader not only that this Model of the Universe is a supreme medieval work of art but that it is in a sense the central work, that in which most particular works were embedded, to which they constantly referred, from which they drew a great deal of their strength.

CHAPTER II

RESERVATIONS

I do not exercise myself in great matters:
which are too high for me.

PSALM CXXXI

To describe the imagined universe which is usually pre-supposed in medieval literature and art is not the same thing as writing a general history of medieval science and philosophy.

The Middle Ages, like most ages, were full of change and controversy. Schools of thought rose, contended, and fell. My account of what I call the Medieval Model ignores all this: ignores even the great change from a pre-dominantly Platonic to a predominantly Aristotelian[1] outlook and the direct conflict between Nominalists and Realists. It does so because these things, however import-ant for the historian of thought, have hardly any effect on the literary level. The Model, as regards those ele-ments in it which poets and artists could utilise, remained stable.

Again, the reader will find that I freely illustrate fea-tures of the Model which I call 'Medieval' from authors who wrote after the close of the Middle Ages; from Spenser, Donne or Milton. I do so because, at many points, the old Model still underlies their work. It was not totally and confidently abandoned till the end of the seventeenth century.

[1] The text of Aristotle in Latin translations (themselves often of Arabic translations) begins to be known in the twelfth century.

13

In every period the Model of the Universe which is accepted by the great thinkers helps to provide what we may call a backcloth for the arts. But this backcloth is highly selective. It takes over from the total Model only what is intelligible to a layman and only what makes some appeal to imagination and emotion. Thus our own backcloth contains plenty of Freud and little of Einstein. The medieval backcloth contains the order and influences of the planets, but not much about epicycles and eccentrics. Nor does the backcloth always respond very quickly to great changes in the scientific and philosophical level.

Furthermore, and apart from actual omissions in the backcloth version of the Model, there will usually be a difference of another kind. We may call it a difference of status. The great masters do not take any Model quite so seriously as the rest of us. They know that it is, after all, only a model, possibly replaceable.

The business of the natural philosopher is to construct theories which will 'save appearances'. Most of us first meet this expression in *Paradise Lost* (VIII, 82) and most of us perhaps originally misunderstood it. Milton is translating σώζειν τὰ φαινόμενα, first used, so far as we know, by Simplicius in his commentary on the Aristotelian *De Caelo*. A scientific theory must 'save' or 'preserve' the appearances, the phenomena, it deals with, in the sense of getting them all in, doing justice to them. Thus, for example, your phenomena are luminous points in the night sky which exhibit such and such movements in relation to one another and in relation to an observer at a particular point, or various chosen points, on the surface of the Earth. Your astronomical theory will be a supposal such that, if it were true, the apparent motions from the point or points of observation would be those you have actually observed. The theory will then have 'got in' or 'saved' the appearances.

But if we demanded no more than that from a theory, science would be impossible, for a lively inventive faculty could devise a good many different supposals which would equally save the phenomena. We have therefore had to supplement the canon of saving the phenomena by another canon—first, perhaps, formulated with full clarity by Occam. According to this second canon we must accept (provisionally) not any theory which saves the phenomena but that theory which does so with the fewest possible assumptions. Thus the two theories (*a*) that the bad bits in Shakespeare were all put in by adapters, and (*b*) that Shakespeare wrote them when he was not at his best, will equally 'save' the appearances. But we already know that there was such a person as Shakespeare and that writers are not always at their best. If scholarship hopes ever to achieve the steady progress of the sciences, we must therefore (provisionally) accept the second theory. If we can explain the bad bits without the assumption of an adapter, we must.

In every age it will be apparent to accurate thinkers that scientific theories, being arrived at in the way I have described, are never statements of fact. That stars appear to move in such and such ways, or that substances behaved thus and thus in the laboratory—these are statements of fact. The astronomical or chemical theory can never be more than provisional. It will have to be abandoned if a more ingenious person thinks of a supposal which would 'save' the observed phenomena with still fewer assumptions, or if we discover new phenomena which it cannot save at all.

This would, I believe, be recognised by all thoughtful scientists today. It was recognised by Newton if, as I am told, he wrote not 'the attraction varies inversely as the square of the distance', but 'all happens as if' it so varied. It was certainly recognised in the Middle Ages. 'In astronomy', says Aquinas, 'an account is given of eccentrics and epicycles on the ground that if their assumption is made (*hac positione facta*) the sensible appearances as regards celestial motions can be saved. But this is not a strict proof (*sufficienter probans*) since for all we know (*forte*) they could also be saved by some different assumption.'[1] The real reason why Copernicus raised no ripple and Galileo raised a storm, may well be that whereas the one offered a new supposal about celestial motions, the other insisted on treating this supposal as fact. If so, the real revolution consisted not in a new theory of the heavens but in 'a new theory of the nature of theory'.[2]

On the highest level, then, the Model was recognised as provisional. What we should like to know is how far down the intellectual scale this cautious view extended.

[1] 1ª XXXII, Art. 1, *ad secundum*.
[2] A. O. Barfield, *Saving the Appearances* (1957), p. 51.

Reservations

In our age I think it would be fair to say that the ease with which a scientific theory assumes the dignity and rigidity of fact varies inversely with the individual's scientific education. In discussion with wholly uneducated audiences I have sometimes found matter which real scientists would regard as highly speculative more firmly believed than many things within our real knowledge; the popular *imago* of the Cave Man ranked as hard fact, and the life of Caesar or Napoleon as doubtful rumour. We must not, however, hastily assume that the situation was quite the same in the Middle Ages. The mass media which have in our time created a popular scientism, a caricature of the true sciences, did not then exist. The ignorant were more aware of their ignorance then than now. Yet I get the impression that when the poets use motives from the Model, they are not aware, as Aquinas was, of its modest epistemological status. I do not mean that they have raised the question he raises and answered it differently. More probably it has never been before their minds. They would have felt that the responsibility for their cosmological, or for their historical or religious, beliefs rested on others. It was enough for them that they were following good *auctours*, great clerks, 'thise olde wise'.

Not only epistemologically but also emotionally the Model probably meant less to the great thinkers than to the poets. This, I believe, must be so in all ages. Quasi-religious responses to the hypostatised abstraction *Life* are to be sought in Shaw or Wells or in a highly poetical philosopher such as Bergson, not in the papers and lectures of biologists. Delight in the Medieval Model is expressed by Dante or Jean de Meung rather than by Albertus and Aquinas. Partly, no doubt, this is because expression, of whatever emotion, is not the business of philosophers. But I suspect this is not the whole story. It is not in the nature of things that great thinkers should take much interest in Models. They have more difficult and more controversial matters in hand. Every Model is a construct of answered questions. The expert is engaged either in raising new questions or in giving new answers to old ones. When he is doing the first, the old, agreed Model is of no interest to him; when he is doing the second, he is beginning an operation which will finally destroy the old Model altogether.

One particular class of experts, the great spiritual writers, ignore the Model almost completely. We need to know something about the Model if we are to read Chaucer, but we can neglect it when we are reading St Bernard or *The Scale of Perfection* or the *Imitation*. This is partly because the spiritual books are entirely practical—like medical books. A man concerned about the state of his soul will not usually be much helped by thinking about the spheres or the structure of the atom. But perhaps there was in the Middle Ages another factor also at work. Their cosmology and their religion were not such easy bedfellows as might be supposed. At first we may fail to notice this, for the cosmology appears to us, in its firmly theistic basis and its ready welcome to the supernatural, to be eminently religious. And so in one sense it is. But it is not eminently Christian. The Pagan elements embedded in it involved a conception of God, and of man's place in the universe, which, if not in logical contradiction to Christianity, were subtly out of harmony with it. There was no direct 'conflict between religion and science' of the nineteenth-century type; but there was an incompatibility of temperament. Delighted contemplation of the Model and intense religious feeling of a specifically Christian character are seldom fused except in the work of Dante.

One difference between describing the Model and writing a history of thought has been, undesignedly, illustrated in the previous chapter. I there cited both Plato and Aristotle: but the role I had to give them was philosophically humiliating—the one called as witness to a scrap of daemonology, the other for some exploded physics. Naturally, I was not suggesting that their real and permanent place in the history of Western thought rested on such foundations. But they concerned us less as great thinkers than as contributors—indirect, unconscious, and almost accidental contributors—to the Model. The history of thought as such would deal chiefly with the influence of great experts upon great experts—the influence, not of Aristotle's physics, but of his ethics and his dialectical method on those of Aquinas. But the Model is built out of the real, or supposed, agreement of any ancient authors—good or bad, philosophers or poets, understood or misunderstood—who happened, for whatever reason, to be available.

These explanations will perhaps set at rest, or re-direct, one doubt which a prospective reader might possibly feel on first dipping here and there into this book. I can imagine such a preliminary reconnaissance leading to the question 'But how far down the intellectual scale did this Model of yours penetrate? Are you not offering as the background for literature things which were really known only to a few experts?' It will now be seen, I hope, that the question 'how far up' the real potency of the Model was operative is at least equally pertinent.

There was no doubt a level below the influence of the Model. There were ditchers and alewives who had not heard of the *Primum Mobile* and did not know that the earth was spherical; not because they thought it was flat but because they did not think about it at all. Nevertheless, elements from the Model appear in such a homely and artless compilation as the *South English Legendary*. On the other hand, as I have tried to indicate, there were certainly levels, both intellectual and spiritual, which were in a sense above the Model's full power.

I say 'in a sense' because these metaphors of *above* and *below* might otherwise carry a false suggestion. It might be supposed that I believe science and philosophy to be somehow intrinsically more valuable than literature and art. I hold no such view. The 'higher' intellectual level is higher only by one particular standard: by another standard the poetic level is higher. Comparative evaluations of essentially different excellences are in my opinion senseless.[1] A surgeon is better than a violinist at operating and a violinist better than a surgeon at playing the violin.

[1] Cf. the maxim (quoted in Coleridge's *Aids to Reflection*) *heterogenea non comparari possunt*.

Reservations

Nor am I at all suggesting that the poets and artists are wrong or stupid in omitting from their backcloth much which the experts think important. An artist needs some anatomy; he need not go on to physiology, much less to biochemistry. And if these sciences change much more than anatomy changes, his work will not reflect their progress.

CHAPTER III

SELECTED MATERIALS:
THE CLASSICAL PERIOD

Oh vana gloria de l'umane posse
com poco verde in su la cima dura.

DANTE

Before turning to the Model itself it will be well to give
an account of some at least among the sources from which
it was derived. To deal with all would be far beyond the
scope of this book and would lead me into regions where
better guides can easily be found. Thus there are perhaps
no sources so necessary for a student of medieval literature
to know as the Bible, Virgil, and Ovid, but I shall say
nothing about any of the three. Many of my readers
know them already; those who do not are at least aware
that they need to. Again, though I shall have much to
say about the old astronomy, I shall not describe Ptolemy's
Almagest. The text, with a French translation,[1] is available
and many histories of science exist. (Casual statements
about pre-Copernican astronomy in modern scientists who
are not historians are often unreliable.) I shall concentrate
on those sources which are least easily accessible or least
generally known to educated people, or which best
illustrate the curious process whereby the Model assimi-
lated them. Those which seem to me most important
belong to the third, fourth and fifth centuries A.D., and

[1] *Mathematikes Suntaxeos*, Greek text and French trans. M. Halma
(Paris, 1913).

these will form the subject of the next chapter. In the meantime I turn to certain earlier works which the 'classical' tradition in our schools has tended to keep in the background.

A. THE 'SOMNIUM SCIPIONIS'[1]

Plato's *Republic*, as everyone knows, ends with an account of the after-life, put into the mouth of one Er the Armenian who had returned from the dead. When Cicero, somewhere about 50 B.C., wrote his own *Republic*, not to be outdone, he ended with a similar vision. Scipio Africanus Minor, one of the speakers in Cicero's dialogue, relates in the sixth and last book a remarkable dream. Most of Cicero's *Republic* has reached us in a fragmentary condition. For a reason which will appear later, this part, the *Somnium Scipionis*, has come down intact.

Scipio begins by telling us that during the evening which preceded his dream he had been talking about his (adoptive) grandfather, Scipio Africanus Major. That, he says, is doubtless why he appeared to me in my dream, for our dreams are commonly begotten by our recent waking thoughts (VI, x). This little attempt to give plausibility to a fictitious dream by offering psychological causes is imitated in the dream-poetry of the Middle Ages. Thus Chaucer in the Proem to the *Book of the Duchesse* reads of lovers parted by death before he dreams of them; in the *Parlement* he reads the *Somnium Scipionis*

[1] Cicero, *De Republica, De Legibus*, text and trans. by C. W. Keyes (Loeb Library, 1928).

itself and suggests that this may be why he dreamed of Scipio (106–8).

Africanus Major carries Africanus Minor up to a height whence he looks down on Carthage 'from an exalted place, bright and shining, filled with stars' (xi). They are in fact in the highest celestial sphere, the *stellatum*. This is the prototype of many ascents to Heaven in later literature: those of Dante, of Chaucer (in the *Hous of Fame*), of Troilus' ghost, of the Lover in the *King's Quair*. Don Quixote and Sancho (II, xli) were once persuaded that they were making just such an ascent.

After foretelling his grandson's future political career (just as Cacciaguida foretells Dante's in *Paradiso*, XVII), Africanus explains to him that 'all who have been saviours or champions of their native land or increased its dominions have their appointed place in Heaven' (xiii). This is a good instance of the intractable material with which later syncretism was confronted. Cicero is making a heaven for public men, for politicians and generals. Neither the Pagan sage (like Pythagoras), nor the Christian saint, could enter it. This was quite inconsistent with some Pagan, and with all Christian, authorities. But in this case, as we shall see later, a harmonistic interpretation had been reached before the Middle Ages began.

The younger Scipio, fired by this prospect, now asks why he should not hasten to join that happy company at once. 'No,' replies the elder (xv), 'unless that God who has for his temple this whole universe which you behold, has set you free from the fetters of the body, the way hither is not open to you. For men were born under the law that they should garrison (*tuerentur*) the globe you see yonder in the middle of the temple, which is called Earth.... Therefore you, Publius, and all good men must retain the soul in the body's fetters and not depart from human life without the orders of him who gave you a soul; otherwise, you may be held to have deserted the duty allotted by God to man.' This prohibition of suicide is Platonic. I think Cicero is following a passage in Plato's *Phaedo* where Socrates remarks of suicide, 'They say it is unlawful' (61ᶜ), even one of those few acts which are unlawful in all circumstances (62ᵃ). He goes on to explain. Whether we accept or not the doctrine taught in the Mysteries (that the body is a prison and we must not break from it), at any rate we men are certainly the property (κτήματα) of the gods, and property must not dispose of itself (62ᵇ⁻ᶜ). That this prohibition makes part of Christian ethics is indisputable; but many, not unlearned, people have been unable to tell me when or how it became so. The passage we are considering may possibly have had some influence. Certainly references in later writers to suicide or to the unlawful risking of one's own life seem to be written with the speech of Africanus in mind, for they draw out the military metaphor which is implicit in it. Spenser's Redcross Knight answers Despair's temptation to suicide with the words

> The souldier may not move from watchfull sted
> Nor leave his stand[1] untill his Captaine bed,

---

[1] In the sense of Latin *statio*, i.e. 'post'.

and Despair, trying to turn the argument, replies

> He that points the Centonell his roome,
> Doth license him depart at sound of morning droome.
>
> (*F.Q.* I, ix, 41.)

Similarly Donne (*Satyre* III, 29) reprobates duelling in the words

> O desperate coward, wilt thou seeme bold, and
> To thy foes and his (who made thee to stand
> Sentinell in his worlds garrison) thus yeeld....

Scipio now noticed that the stars were globes which easily outstripped the Earth in size. Indeed the Earth now appeared so small in comparison that the Roman Empire, which was hardly more than a point on that tiny surface, excited his contempt (xvi). This passage was constantly in the minds of succeeding writers. The insignificance (by cosmic standards) of the Earth became as much a commonplace to the medieval, as to the modern, thinker; it was part of the moralists' stock-in-trade, used, as Cicero uses it (xix), to mortify human ambition.

Other details from the *Somnium* will meet us in later literature, though it was certainly not the only channel by which all of them were transmitted. In xviii we have the music of the spheres; in xxvi, the doctrine of the earth-bound ghost. In xvii (if it will not be thought too trifling) we may notice that the Sun is the world's mind, *mens mundi*. Ovid (*Met.* IV, 228) made it *mundi oculus*, the world's eye. The elder Pliny (*Nat. Hist.* II, iv) reverted to Cicero with a slight change: *mundi animus*. Bernardus Silvestris used both honorifics—*mens mundi...mun-*

danusque oculus.[1] Milton, who had presumably not read
Bernardus but had certainly read the *Somnium* and Ovid
and probably Pliny, does the same, 'Thou Sun, of this
great world both eye and soul' (*P.L.* v, 171). Shelley,
perhaps with Milton only in mind, raises the eye image to
a higher level: 'the eye with which the universe Beholds
itself and knows itself divine' (*Hymn of Apollo*, 31).

Far more important than such curiosities, however, is
the general character of this text, which is typical of much
material which the Middle Ages inherited from antiquity.
Superficially it seems to need only a few touches to bring
it into line with Christianity; fundamentally it pre-
supposes a wholly Pagan ethics and metaphysics. As we
have seen, there is a heaven, but a heaven for statesmen.
Scipio is exhorted (xxiii) to look above and despise the
world; but he is to despise primarily 'the talk of the
rabble' and what he is to look for above is the reward
'of his achievements' (*rerum*). It will be *decus*, fame or
'glory' in a sense very different from the Christian.
Most deceptive of all is xxiv, where he is exhorted to
remember that not he, but only his body, is mortal.
Every Christian would in some sense agree. But it is
followed almost immediately by the words 'Realise therefore that you are a god'. For Cicero that is obvious;
'among the Greeks', says Von Hügel—and he might
have said 'in all classical thought'—'he who says *immortal*
says *god*. The conceptions are interchangeable.'[2] If men
can go to heaven it is because they came from there; their

---

[1] *De Mundi Universitate*, II, *Pros.* v, p. 44, ed. Barach and Wrobel
(Innsbruck, 1876).   [2] *Eternal Life*, I, iii.

ascent is a return (*revertuntur*, xxvi). That is why the body is 'fetters'; we come into it by a sort of Fall. It is irrelevant to our nature; 'the mind of each man is the man' (xxiv). All this belongs to a circle of ideas wholly different from the Christian doctrines of man's creation, fall, redemption, and resurrection. The attitude to the body which it involves was to be an unfortunate legacy for medieval Christendom.

Cicero also hands on a doctrine which may have helped, for centuries, to discourage geographical exploration. The Earth is (of course) spherical. It is divided into five zones, of which two, the Arctic and the Antarctic, are uninhabitable through cold. Between the two habitable and temperate zones spreads the torrid zone, uninhabitable through heat. That is why the Antipodes, the 'contrariwise-footed' people who 'plant their footsteps in the direction opposite to you' (*adversa vobis urgent vestigia*), and live in the southern temperate zone, are nothing to us. We can never meet them; a belt of deadly heat is between us and them (xx). It was against this theory that George Best wrote his chapter 'Experiences and reasons of the Sphere, to proove all parts of the worlde habitable, and thereby to confute the position[1] of the five Zones' (*A True Discourse*, 1578).

Like all his successors, Cicero makes the Moon the boundary between eternal and perishable things, and also asserts the influence of the planets on our fortunes—rather vaguely and incompletely but also without the qualifications which a medieval theologian would have added (xvii).

[1] I.e. doctrine, theorem.

Selected Materials: the Classical Period

B. LUCAN

Lucan lived from A.D. 34 to 65. Seneca and Gallio (the one who 'cared for none of these things') were his uncles. His epic on the Civil War, the *Pharsalia*, was cut short by the wretchedest death a man can die; he conspired against Nero, was caught, turned king's evidence under a promise of pardon, incriminated (among many) his own mother, and was executed none the less. His poem is now, in my opinion, undervalued; it is, to be sure, a blood and thunder affair, but no worse in that respect than Webster and Tourneur. In style, Lucan is, like Young, 'a gloomy epigrammatist', and like Seneca, a master of 'the verbal *coup de théâtre*'.

This style was not, so far as I know, imitated in the Middle Ages, but Lucan was regarded with great respect. Dante in the *De Volgari Eloquentia* mentions him, along with Virgil, Ovid, and Statius as one of the four *regulati poetae* (II, vi, 7). In the noble castle of Limbo he ranks side by side with Homer, Horace, Ovid, Virgil, and Dante himself.[1] Chaucer, sending his *Troilus* out into the world, bids it kiss the footprints of 'Virgile, Ovyde, Omer, Lucan, and Stace' (v, 1791).

The most popular of Lucan's figures was Amyclas,[2] the poor fisherman who ferries Caesar from Palaestra to Italy. Lucan uses him as a peg on which to hang the

[1] *Inferno*, IV, 88.
[2] See E. R. Curtius, *European Literature and the Latin Middle Ages*, trans. W. R. Trask (London, 1953). Unfortunately the translations of Latin quotations in the English version of this book are not to be relied on.

praise of poverty. Amyclas, he says, was not at all discomposed by Caesar knocking at his door: what temples, what ramparts, could boast the like security (v, 527 *sq.*)? Dante translates the passage enthusiastically in the *Convivio* (IV, xiii, 12), and recalls it more beautifully in the *Paradiso* when he makes Thomas Aquinas say that the bride of St Francis had long remained without a suitor despite the fact that he who frightened all the world beside found her unalarmed in the house of Amyclas (XI, 67 *sq.*). Two of Lucan's great ladies, Julia (from *Pharsalia*, I, 111), and Marcia (II, 326) also appear among the noble and virtuous Pagans in the *Inferno* (IV, 128). The *Corniglia* there associated with them is often taken to be the mother of the Gracchi, but I think she is more probably Cornelia the wife of Pompey who appears in Lucan (v, 722 *sq.*) as an ideal spouse.

Except as evidence of Lucan's popularity, however, these borrowings do not much concern us. Two other passages in Dante are for our purpose far more instructive, because they reveal the peculiarities of the medieval approach to ancient texts.

In his second book (325 *sq.*) Lucan relates how Marcia, first married to Cato and then, at his command, to Hortensius, now after Hortensius' death returns to her old husband at his and Rome's darkest hour, and demands, successfully, a re-marriage. Though rhetorically treated, it is a moving, and a purely human scene. But Dante[1] reads it all allegorically. *Marcia* is for him *la nobile anima.* As a virgin she represents *l'adolescenza*; as Cato's

[1] *Convivio*, IV, xxviii, 13 *sq.*

wife, *la gioventute*. The children she bore to Cato are the virtues proper to that period of life. Her marriage to Hortensius is *senettude* and her children by him the virtues of the elderly. The death of Hortensius and her widowhood represent the transition to extreme old age (*senio*). Her return to Cato shows us the noble soul turning to God. 'And', adds Dante, 'what earthly man was worthier than Cato to symbolise (*significare*) God? Assuredly none.' This astonishingly high estimate of the old suicide helps to explain his later position as usher to Purgatory in the *Comedy*.

Again, in the same *Convivio* (III, v, 12), Dante asserts the existence of the Antipodes, and very naturally quotes Albertus Magnus—as good a scientific authority as was then available—in support of his view. But the interesting thing is that, not content with this, he also cites Lucan. During the desert march in *Pharsalia*, IX, one of the soldiers, complaining that they were lost in an unknown region of the earth, had said, 'And perhaps Rome herself is now under our feet' (877). The poet is ranked with the scientist as authority for a purely scientific proposition. This astonishing failure or refusal to distinguish—in practice, though not always in theory—between books of different sorts must be borne in mind whenever we are trying to gauge the total effect of an ancient text on its medieval readers. The habit, like many medieval habits, long outlived the Middle Ages. Burton is a notable offender. He illustrates[1] the physiological force of imagination from the *Aethiopica* of Heliodorus as if that

[1] Pt. I, 2, M. 3, subs. 2.

romance were a history, and offers us the myth of
Orpheus as evidence that beasts can appreciate music.[1]
In the long Latin passage on sexual perversions[2] Pygma-
lion and Pasiphae are mentioned side by side with modern
and historical instances. It is therefore quite possible that
Lucan's lengthy account of the abominations practised by
the witch Erictho[3] may have had a more than literary,
and a most disastrous, influence. Witch-hunting tribunals
might have had it in mind. But since the great period of
witch hunts fell after the Middle Ages, I will not here
explore the possibility.

What is perhaps Lucan's most important contribution
to the Model comes at the beginning of his ninth book,
where the soul of Pompey ascends from the funeral pyre
to the heavens. This repeats the ascension of Scipio in
Cicero's *Dream*, adding new details. Pompey arrives
'where the murky air joins the star-bearing wheels',[4] the
spheres (5). That is, he has come to the great frontier
between air and aether, between Aristotle's 'Nature' and
'Sky'. This is clearly at the orbit of the moon, for the
region of the air is 'what lies between the countries of
Earth and the lunar movements',[5] (6), inhabited by
semidei Manes (7), the ghosts of good men who are now
demigods. Apparently they inhabit the very surface of
the air, almost in the aether itself, for Lucan describes
them as *patientes aetheris imi* (8), 'able to bear (perhaps to

---

[1] Pt. II, M. 2, 6, subs. 3.   [2] Pt. III, 2, M. 1, subs. 2.

[3] *Pharsalia*, VI, 507 *sq.*

[4] *Qua niger astriferis connectitur axibus aer.*

[5] *Quodque patet terras inter lunaeque meatus.*

breathe), the lowest aether', as if the aether grew more airish or the air more aetherial at their meeting-place. Here first Pompey fills himself with, drinks in, 'true light'[1] (11, 12) and sees 'under how vast a night lies what we call Day'[2] (13). Finally *risitque sui ludibria trunci* (14): he looked down and saw the mockeries done to his own corpse, which was having a wretched and hugger-mugger funeral. They made him laugh.

Every detail of this will meet us again in one author or another; for Englishmen the passage, as is well known, has another and more particular interest. First, Boccaccio borrowed it in his *Teseide* (XI, 1 *sq.*) and used it for the ghost of his Arcita. It went flying up to the concavity of the eighth sphere or *stellatum*, leaving behind it the convex sides (*conversi*) of the (other) *elementi*—which here, as often, are not elements but celestial spheres. Each sphere was naturally concave as he came up to it from beneath and convex when he looked back on it from above. That of the Fixed Stars, the *stellatum*, remains concave because he does not go through and beyond it (he has already gone far higher than Pompey). Like Scipio, he observes how very small the Earth is; like Pompey, he laughs; but not because his funeral, like Pompey's, is a hole-and-corner affair: it is the mourning that he laughs at. Chaucer ignored this passage when he was using the *Teseide* for his

[1] *Se lumine vero Implevit.*

[2] *Quanta sub nocte iaceret Nostra dies.* I think this might mean *either* 'How dark, compared with the aether, our terrestrial day is', *or* 'Under how huge an abyss of nocturnal phenomena (stars, see 11, 12, 13) our terrestrial day takes place'. Much more probably the former, see below, p. 111.

Knight's Tale, but used it for the ghost of Troilus (v, 1807 *sq.*). Some have taken the laughter of Troilus to be embittered and ironic. I never thought so, and the descent of the passage, as we have just traced it, seems to me to make it even less probable. I think all three ghosts—Pompey's, Arcita's, and Troilus'—laughed for the same reason, laughed at the littleness of all those things that had seemed so important before they died; as we laugh, on waking, at the trifles or absurdities that loomed so large in our dreams.

C. STATIUS, CLAUDIAN, AND THE LADY 'NATURA'

Statius, whose *Thebaid* appeared in the 'nineties of the first century, ranked in the Middle Ages (as we have already seen) with Virgil, Homer, and Lucan. Like Lucan, he strained after the stunning phrase, less successfully, but also less continuously. He had a larger mind than Lucan, more true seriousness, more pity, a more versatile imagination; the *Thebaid* is a less tiring and a more spacious poem than the *Pharsalia*. The Middle Ages were quite right to accept it as a noble 'historial' romance. It was in many ways especially congenial to them. Its Jupiter was more like the God of monotheism than any other being in the Pagan poetry they knew. Its fiends (and some of its gods) were more like the devils of their own religion than any other Pagan spirits. Its deep respect for virginity—with even the curious suggestion that the sexual act, however sanctioned by marriage, is a *culpa* which needs excuse (II, 233, 256)—appealed to the

vein of asceticism in their theology. Finally, the vividness
and importance of its personifications (*Virtus, Clementia,
Pietas,* and *Natura*) brought it in places very close to the
fully allegorical poetry in which they delighted. But I
have shot my bolt about these matters elsewhere[1] and at
present *Natura* is my only concern.

The reader of Renaissance and Medieval literature will
have met this lady or goddess fairly often. He will recall
the veiled and numinous Nature of Spenser (*F.Q.,
Mutabilitie,* vii); going back from her, he will meet the
more genial, but hardly less august, Nature in Chaucer's
Parlement. In Deguileville's *Pèlerinage* he will be sur-
prised by a Nature more sturdy and turbulent than
either; a Nature with more than a dash of the Wife of
Bath in her, who sets her arms akimbo and stands up to a
superior power in defence of her lawful franchises.[2] Still
re-ascending, he will come to the Nature who dominates
the *Romance of the Rose* for thousands of lines (15,893–
19,438); as vivid as Deguileville's, as genial as Chaucer's,
hardly less divine than Spenser's, but far more purposive,
far busier, than all of them; working unwearied in her
contest with death; weeping, repenting, complaining, con-
fessing, receiving penance and absolution; of a beauty
that the poet cannot describe, for in her God set the
inexhaustible fountain of all beauty (16,232); an image of
energy and fertility which at moments (Jean de Meung is
fatally digressive) takes one's breath away. From her it is
only a step back to *Natura* as Alanus brings her in, stiffly

[1] *The Allegory of Love*, pp. 49 *sq.*; 'Dante's Statius', *Medium Aevum*,
xxv, 3.   [2] In Lydgate's version, 3344 *sq.*

robed in rhetoric, conceit, and symbol, pleading again the cause of life or procreation in her *planctus* (against the sodomites); and thence to the two figures of *Physis* and *Natura* who are the heroines of that more sober work, Bernardus' *De Mundi Universitate*. For all this the student will quite rightly suspect a classical origin. When he turns to those ancients whom the Middle Ages knew he will find what he is looking for. But he will not find very much of it. The medieval development, in quantity and still more in vitality, is quite out of proportion to the hints supplied by antiquity.

He will find nothing (where he might hope to find it) in Plato's *Timaeus*. The passages in Marcus Aurelius where *Physis* is addressed as a deity will be no use, for they were unknown in the Middle Ages. The relevant material comes down to not much more than Statius and Claudian.[1] In Statius *Natura* is seldom mentioned, but the passages are impressive. In XI, 465 *sq.*, she is the *princeps* and *creatrix*, I think, of all things, certainly of that very passion (*Pietas*) which rebels against her. In XII, 645, she is the *dux* of those who are fighting a holy war against things monstrous and 'unnatural'. In Claudian we get a little more. She is the demiurge who reduced primeval chaos to cosmos (*De Raptu Proserpinae*, I, 249); she appointed the gods to serve Jupiter (*De IV° Consulatu Honorii*, 198 *sq.*); more memorably, she sits, aged yet beautiful, before the cavern of *Aevum* in the *De Consulatu Stilichonis* (II, 424 *sq.*).

[1] Passages which can be quoted from Cicero, Chalcidius, and doubtless many others, show only a momentary (metaphorical, not allegorical) personification of *Natura*—such a personification as any important abstract noun is likely to undergo.

Why the ancients made so little of Nature, and the medievals so much, may be easier to understand after a glance at her history.

Nature may be the oldest of things, but *Natura* is the youngest of deities. Really ancient mythology knows nothing of her. It seems to me impossible that such a figure could ever arise in a genuinely mythopoeic age; what we call 'nature-worship' has never heard of what we call 'Nature'. 'Mother' Nature is a conscious metaphor. 'Mother' Earth is something quite different. All earth, contrasted with all the sky, can be, indeed must be, intuited as a unity. The marriage relation between Father Sky (or Dyaus) and Mother Earth forces itself on the imagination. He is on top, she lies under him. He does things to her (shines and, more important, rains upon her, into her): out of her, in response, come forth the crops— just as calves come out of cows or babies out of wives. In a word, he begets, she bears. You can see it happening. This is genuine mythopoeia. But while the mind is working on that level, what, in heaven's name, is Nature? Where is she? Who has seen her? What does she do?

The pre-Socratic philosophers of Greece invented Nature. They first had the idea (a much odder one than the veil of immemorial familiarity usually allows us to realise) that the great variety of phenomena which surrounds us could all be impounded under a name and talked about as a single object. Later thinkers took over the name and the implication of unity which (like every name) it carried. But they sometimes used it to cover less than everything; hence Aristotle's Nature which covers only the sublunary. In that way, the concept of Nature unexpectedly rendered possible a clear conception of the Supernatural (Aristotle's God is as supernatural as anything could be). The object (if it is an object) called 'Nature' could be personified. And this personification could be either treated as a mere colour of rhetoric or seriously accepted as a goddess. That is why the goddess appears so late, long after the real mythopoeic state of mind has passed away. You cannot have the goddess Nature till you have the concept 'Nature', and you cannot have the concept until you have begun to abstract.

But as long as the concept covers everything, the goddess (who personifies the concept) is necessarily a jejune and inactive deity; for everything is not a subject about which anything of much interest can be said. All her religious, and all her poetic, vitality depends on making her something less than everything. If she is at times the object of real religious feeling in Marcus Aurelius, that is because he contrasts or confronts her with the finite individual—with his own rebellious and recalcitrant self. If in Statius she has moments of poetic life, that is because she is opposed to something better than her self (*Pietas*) or something worse (the unnatural, such as incest and fratricide). Of course there are philosophical difficulties about this opposing to the goddess Nature things which the concept Nature must certainly include. We may leave Stoics and other Pantheists to get out of this scrape as best they can. The point is that the medieval poets were not in the scrape at all. They believed from the outset that Nature was not everything. She was created. She was not God's highest, much less His only, creature. She had her proper place, below the Moon. She had her appointed duties as God's vicegerent in that area. Her own lawful subjects, stimulated by rebel angels, might disobey her and become 'unnatural'. There were things above her, and things below. It is precisely this limitation and subordination of Nature which sets her free for her triumphant poetical career. By surrendering the dull claim to be everything, she becomes somebody. Yet all the while she is, for the medievals, only a personification. A figurative being on these terms is apparently more potent than a deity really believed in who, by being all things, is almost nothing.

Before leaving Statius I cannot forbear adding a paragraph (which the incurious are invited to skip) on a mere curiosity. In the fourth Book of the *Thebaid* he alludes to a deity he will not name—'the sovereign of the threefold world' (516). The same anonymous power is probably meant in Lucan's *Pharsalia* (VI, 744) where the witch, conjuring a reluctant ghost back into the corpse, threatens it with Him

quo numquam terra vocato
Non concussa tremit, qui Gorgona cernit apertam.[1]

Lactantius in his commentary on the *Thebaid* says that Statius 'means δημιουργόν, the god whose name it is unlawful to know'. This is plain sailing: the demiurge (workman) being the Creator in the *Timaeus*. But there are two variants in the manuscripts; one is *demogorgona*,

[1] At whose pronouncèd name earth never failed To tremble, who alone dares see unveiled The Gorgon's face.

the other *demogorgon*. From the latter of these corruptions later ages evolved a completely new deity, Demogorgon, who was to enjoy a distinguished literary career in Boccaccio's *Genealogy of the Gods*, in Spenser, in Milton, and in Shelley. This is perhaps the only time a scribal blunder underwent an apotheosis.

D. APULEIUS, 'DE DEO SOCRATIS'

Apuleius, born in Numidia about 125 A.D., is now usually (and deservedly) remembered for his curious romance, the *Metamorphoses* or *Golden Ass*. For a medievalist, however, his essay *On the god of Socrates* is more important.

Two passages from Plato underlie it. One is in the *Apology* (31^{c-d}), where Socrates explains why he abstained from political life. 'The reason', he says, 'is one you have often heard me mention. Something divine and daemoniac (θεῖόν τι καὶ δαιμόνιον) happens to me.... It has been so ever since I was a boy. There comes a voice which, whenever I hear it, always forbids something I am about to do, but never commands.'[1]

'God' and 'daemon', as present here in their adjectives 'divine' and 'daemoniac', may be synonyms, as, I take it, they often are for other Greek writers both in prose and verse. But in the second passage (*Symposium*, 202^{e}–203^{e}), Plato draws a clear distinction between them which was to be influential for centuries. Daemons are there creatures of a middle nature between gods and men—like Milton's 'Middle spirits—Betwixt the angelical and human kind'.[2]

[1] Cf. *Phaedrus*, 242^{b-c}. [2] *P.L.* III, 461.

Through these intermediaries, and through them alone, we mortals have any intercourse with the gods. For θεὸς ἀνθρώπῳ οὐ μίγνυται; as Apuleius translates it, *nullus deus miscetur hominibus*, no god converses with men. The voice that spoke to Socrates was that of a daemon, not a god.

About these 'middle spirits' or daemons Apuleius has much to tell us. They naturally inhabit the middle region between Earth and aether; that is, the air—which extends upwards as far as the orbit of the Moon. All is, in fact, so arranged 'that every part of nature may have its appropriate animals'. At first sight, he admits, we might suppose that birds provide the 'appropriate animals' for the air. But they are quite inadequate: they do not ascend above the higher mountain-tops. *Ratio* demands that there should be a species genuinely native to the air, as gods are to the aether and men to the Earth. I should be hard put to it to choose any single English word as the right translation of *ratio* in this context. 'Reason', 'method', 'fitness', and 'proportion' might all put in a claim.

The daemons have bodies of a finer consistency than clouds, which are not normally visible to us. It is because they have bodies that he calls them animals: obviously, he does not mean that they are beasts. They are rational (aerial) animals, as we are rational (terrestrial) animals, and the gods proper are rational (aetherial) animals. The idea that even the highest created spirits—the gods, as distinct from God—were, after their own fashion, incarnate, had some sort of material 'vehicle', goes back to Plato. He had called the true gods, the deified stars, 3ῷα, animals.[1] Scholasticism, in regarding the angels—which is what the gods or aetherial creatures are called in Christian language—as pure or naked spirits, was revolutionary. The Florentine Platonists reverted to the older view.

The daemons are 'between' us and the gods not only locally and materially but qualitatively as well. Like the impassible gods, they are immortal: like mortal men, they are passible (xiii). Some of them, before they became daemons, lived in terrestrial bodies; were in fact men. That is why Pompey saw *semidei Manes*, demigod-ghosts, in the airy region. But this is not true of all daemons. Some, such as Sleep and Love, were never human. From this class an individual daemon (or *genius*, the standard Latin translation of *daemon*) is allotted to each human being as his 'witness and guardian' through life (xvi). It would detain us too long here to trace the steps whereby a man's *genius*, from being an invisible, personal, and external attendant, became his true self, and then his cast of mind, and finally (among the Romantics) his literary or artistic gifts. To understand this process fully would be to grasp that great movement of internalisation, and that consequent aggrandisement of man and desiccation of the outer universe, in which the psychological history of the West has so largely consisted.[2]

Apart from its direct contributions to the Model, this

[1] *Timaeus*, 38ᵉ.
[2] For another, and very different, sense of *genius*, see my *Allegory of Love*, Appendix I.

little work has a twofold value for those who are embarking on medieval studies.

In the first place, it illustrates the sort of channel through which scraps of Plato—often scraps which were very marginal and unimportant in Plato's own work—trickled down to the Middle Ages. Of Plato himself they had little more than an incomplete Latin version of a single dialogue, the *Timaeus*. That by itself, perhaps, would hardly have sufficed to produce a 'Platonic period'. But they also received a diffused Platonism, inextricably mixed with neo-Platonic elements, indirectly, through such authors as Apuleius and those whom we shall be considering in the next chapter. These, with the *Platonici* whom St Augustine read[1] (Latin translators of the neo-Platonists), provided the intellectual atmosphere in which the new Christian culture grew up. The 'Platonism' of the early ages was therefore something very different from that either of the Renaissance or of the nineteenth century.

In the second place, Apuleius introduces us to two principles—unless, indeed, they are really the same principle—which will meet us again and again as we proceed.

One is what I call the Principle of the Triad. The clearest statement of it in Plato himself comes from the *Timaeus*: 'it is impossible that two things only should be joined together without a third. There must be some bond in between both to bring them together' (31^{b-c}). The principle is not stated but assumed in the assertion of the

[1] *Confessions*, VII, ix.

Symposium that god does not meet man. They can encounter one another only indirectly; there must be some wire, some medium, some introducer, some bridge—a third thing of some sort—in between them. Daemons fill the gap. We shall find Plato himself, and the medievals, endlessly acting on their principle; supplying bridges, as it were, 'third things'—between reason and appetite, soul and body, king and commons.

The other is the Principle of Plenitude. If, between aether and Earth, there is a belt of air, then, it seems to Apuleius, *ratio* herself demands that it should be inhabited. The universe must be fully exploited. Nothing must go to waste.[1]

[1] On this, see A. O. Lovejoy, *The Great Chain of Being* (Harvard, 1957).

CHAPTER IV

SELECTED MATERIALS:
THE SEMINAL PERIOD

And oute of olde feldes as men seith
Cometh at this newe corn.

CHAUCER

All the texts we have hitherto looked at belong unambiguously to the old world, to Pagan antiquity. We
now turn to the transitional period, which can be regarded
as beginning, very roughly, with the birth of Plotinus in
205, and ending with the first datable reference to pseudo-
Dionysius in 533. This was the age which brought the
characteristically medieval frame of mind into being. It also
witnessed the last stand of Paganism and the final triumph
of the Church. Cardinal dates in that story are: 324, when
Constantine urged his subjects to embrace Christianity;
331–3, the reign of Julian and his attempted Pagan revival;
384, when the elder Symmachus pleaded in vain that the
altar of Victory should be restored to the Senate House;
and 390, when Theodosius forbade all Pagan worship.

In a prolonged war the troops on both sides may
imitate one another's methods and catch one another's
epidemics; they may even occasionally fraternise. So in
this period. The conflict between the old and the new
religion was often bitter, and both sides were ready to use
coercion when they dared. But at the same time the
influence of the one upon the other was very great.
During these centuries much that was of Pagan origin

was built irremovably into the Model. It is characteristic of the age that more than one of the works I shall mention has sometimes raised a doubt whether its author was Pagan or Christian.

The precise nature and even, in some senses, the width of the chasm which separated the religions can easily be mistaken if we take our ideas solely from political or ecclesiastical histories: still more, if we take them from more popular sources. Cultured people on both sides had had the same education, read the same poets, learned the same rhetoric. As was shown sixty-odd years ago,[1] social relations between them were sometimes friendly.

I have read a novel which represents all the Pagans of that day as carefree sensualists, and all the Christians as savage ascetics. It is a grave error. They were in some ways far more like each other than either was like a modern man. The leaders on both sides were mono-theists, and both admitted almost an infinity of super-natural beings between God and man. Both were highly intellectual, but also (by our standards) highly super-stitious. The last champions of Paganism were not the sort of men that Swinburne, or a modern 'Humanist', would wish them to have been. They were not lusty extroverts recoiling in horror or contempt from a world 'grown grey' with the breath of the 'pale Galilaean'. If they wanted to get back 'the laurel, the palms, and the paean', it was on most serious and religious grounds. If they longed to see 'the breasts of the nymph in the brake',

[1] S. Dill, *Roman Society in the Last Century of the Western Empire* (1898), cap. I.

46

their longing was not like a satyr's; it was much more like a spiritualist's. A world-renouncing, ascetic, and mystical character then marked the most eminent Pagans no less than their Christian opponents. It was the spirit of the age. Everywhere, on both sides, men were turning away from the civic virtues and the sensual pleasures to seek an inner purgation and a supernatural goal. The modern who dislikes the Christian Fathers would have disliked the Pagan philosophers equally, and for similar reasons. Both alike would have embarrassed him with stories of visions, ecstasies, and apparitions. Between the lower and more violent manifestations of both religions he would have found it hard to choose. To a modern eye (and nostril) Julian with his long nails and densely populated beard might have seemed very like an unwashed monk out of the Egyptian desert.

It will occur to everyone that in an age of conflict those authors whose allegiance has been doubted may have deliberately made it doubtful through caution. This is always a possible hypothesis, but not a necessary one. Where so much ground was—or at least seemed to be—common, a writer could sincerely produce much that was acceptable to many Christian and many Pagan readers alike, provided his work was not explicitly theological. The remoter religious implications of philosophical positions were not always grasped. Hence what we might take to be the difference between a clearly Christian and a possibly Pagan work may really be the difference between a thesis offered, so to speak, to the Faculty of Philosophy and one offered to that of Divinity. This seems to me to be the best explanation of the gulf that separates Boethius' *De Consolatione* from the doctrinal pieces which are (I presume, rightly) attributed to him.

On its highest level the Pagan resistance can almost be identified with the neo-Platonic school. In it the great names are those of Plotinus (205–70), Porphyry (233–304?), Iamblichus (*ob.* 330), and Proclus (*ob.* 485). The first was a genius of the highest order, but Porphyry—and even he often indirectly—was the principal influence in the West. The whole school, while partly a spontaneous development of the Greek genius, seems to me to be also a deliberate response to the challenge of Christianity and, in that respect, indebted to it. In it the last Pagans are carefully dissociating themselves from popular polytheism and saying in effect, 'We too have an explanation of the whole universe. We too have a systematic theology. We, no less than you, have a rule of life—have saints, miracles, devotions, and the hope of union with the Highest.'

The present study, however, is interested not in the short-lived impact of the new religion on the old but with the enduring effect of the old upon the new. The last, and neo-Platonic, wave of Paganism which had gathered up into itself much from the preceding waves, Aristotelian, Platonic, Stoic, and what not, came far inland and made brackish lakes which have, perhaps, never been drained. Not all Christians at all times have detected them or admitted their existence: and among those who have done so there have always been two attitudes. There was then, and is still, a Christian 'left', eager to detect and anxious to banish every Pagan element; but also a Christian 'right' who, like St Augustine, could find the doctrine of the Trinity foreshadowed in the *Platonici*,[1] or could claim triumphantly, like Justin Martyr, 'Whatever things have been well said by all men belong to us Christians'.[2]

A. CHALCIDIUS

The work of Chalcidius[3] is an incomplete translation of Plato's *Timaeus* stopping at the end of 53[b] (that is, about halfway through) and a much longer *commentarius*. This is hardly what we should call a commentary, for it ignores many difficulties and expatiates freely on matters about which Plato had little or nothing to say.

It is dedicated to one Osius or Hosius, who has been identified, not very certainly, with a Bishop of Cordova who attended the Council of Nicaea (325). Even if the identification is correct, this would not enable us to date the work very closely, for we are told by Isidore that the Bishop lived to be over a hundred.

The religion of Chalcidius has been questioned. In favour of his Christianity we note:

(1) The dedication to Osius (always assuming that he really was the Bishop).

(2) He calls the biblical account of Adam's creation 'the teaching of a holier sect' (*sectae sanctioris*).[4]

(3) After glancing at a supposed astrological doctrine in Homer, he mentions the star of the Nativity as some-

---

[1] *Confessions*, VII, ix.   [2] *Apology*, II, xiii.
[3] *Platonis Timaeus interprete Chalcidio*, ed. Z. Wrobel (Lipsiae, 1876).
[4] *Op. cit.* LV, p. 122.

thing vouched for by 'a holier and more venerable story'.[1]

(4) He describes himself as deriving from 'the divine law' truths to which Plato had been guided 'by the impulse (*instinctus*) of truth herself'.[2]

On the other hand:

(1) When he draws on the Old Testament, instead of calling it 'the sacred writings', he usually says merely that he is following the *Hebraei*.[3]

(2) As witnesses to the benefits we mortals have received from good daemons he summons 'all Greeks, Latins and barbarians' (*cuncta Graecia, omne Latium, omnisque Barbaria*).[4] This is a sharp contrast with St Augustine's[5] view that all the daemons of Paganism were evil—were 'demons' in the later sense of the word.

(3) In one place he treats the divine inspiration of Moses as something open to doubt (*ut ferunt*).[6]

(4) He cites Homer, Hesiod, and Empedocles as if they were no less to be taken into account than the sacred writers.

(5) He describes Providence as *Nous* (Mind), a being which holds the second place after the *summus deus* by whom it is perfected as it perfects all other things.[7] This is very much more like the neo-Platonic Trinity than the Christian.

(6) He discusses at great length whether *silva* (matter)

[1] CXXVI, p. 191.
[2] CLXXVI, p. 225.
[3] CXXXII, p. 195; CCC, p. 329.
[4] CXXXII, p. 195.
[5] *De Civitate*, VIII, 14–X, 32.
[6] Chalcidius CCLXXVI, p. 306.
[7] CLXXVI, p. 226.

is inherently evil,[1] without once mentioning the Christian doctrine that God made all things and pronounced them very good.

(7) He wholly rejects the anthropocentric cosmology of Genesis in which the heavenly bodies were made 'to give light upon the earth'. He holds it would be absurd to suppose that the 'blessed and eternal' things above the Moon were ordered for the sake of the perishable things below.[2]

The two last items are less evidential than we might at first suppose. Though Christians were logically bound to admit the goodness of matter that doctrine was not heartily relished; then, and for centuries, the language of some spiritual writers was hardly to be reconciled with it. And I think that there remained throughout the Middle Ages an unresolved discord between those elements in their religion which tended to an anthropocentric view and those in the Model which made man a marginal—almost, as we shall see, a suburban—creature.

For the rest, I think Chalcidius is a Christian, writing philosophically. What he accepted as matters of faith were excluded, as matters of faith, from his thesis. Biblical writers might therefore appear in his work as eminent authors to be taken into account like any other eminent authors, but not treated as the 'oracles of God'. That would have been contrary to the rules of his art: he could be a methodological purist, as we shall see later. Of the deep discrepancy between his neo-Platonic Trinity and the fully Christian doctrine I believe him to have been unaware.

[1] CCLXXXVIII–CCXCVIII, pp. 319–27.　　[2] LXXVI, p. 144.

By translating so much of the *Timaeus* and thus transmitting it to centuries in which little else of Plato was known, Chalcidius determined what the name of Plato should chiefly stand for throughout the Middle Ages. The *Timaeus* has none of the erotic mysticism we find in the *Symposium* or the *Phaedrus*, and almost nothing about politics. And though the Ideas (or Forms) are mentioned, their real place in Plato's theory of knowledge is not displayed. For Chalcidius they become 'ideas' almost in the modern sense; thoughts in the mind of God.[1] It thus came about that, for the Middle Ages, Plato was not the logician, nor the philosopher of love, nor the author of the *Republic*. He was, next to Moses, the great monotheistic cosmogonist, the philosopher of creation; hence, paradoxically, the philosopher of that Nature which the real Plato so often disparaged. To that extent, Chalcidius unconsciously supplied a corrective for the *contemptus mundi* inherent in neo-Platonism and early Christianity alike. It was later to prove fruitful.

As his choice of the *Timaeus* was momentous, so was the fashion in which he treated it. His admitted principle of interpretation was one which makes an author more liable to be misrepresented the more he is revered. In hard places, he holds, we must always attribute to Plato whatever sense appears 'worthiest the wisdom of so great an authority';[2] which inevitably means that all the dominant ideas of the commentator's own age will be read into him.

Plato clearly said (42^b) that the souls of wicked men

[1] CCCIV, p. 333.　　　　[2] CCCII, p. 330.

may be re-incarnated as women, and if that doesn't cure them, finally as beasts. But we are not, says Chalcidius, to suppose that he meant it literally. He only means that, by indulging your passions, you will, in this present life, become more and more like an animal.[1]

In *Timaeus* 40ᵈ–41ᵃ Plato, after describing how God created the gods—not the mythological ones but those he really believed in, the animated stars—asks what is to be said about the popular pantheon. He first degrades them from the rank of gods to that of daemons. He then proceeds, in words almost certainly ironical, to decline any further discussion of them. It is, he says, 'A task quite beyond me. We must accept what was said about them by our ancestors who, according to their own account, were actually their descendants. Surely they must have been well informed about their own progenitors! And who could disbelieve the children of gods?' Chalcidius takes all this *au pied de la lettre*. By telling us to believe our forebears Plato is reminding us that *credulitas* must precede all instruction. And if he declines to discuss further the nature of daemons, this is not, for Chalcidius, because he thought the subject was not a philosopher's business. What he suggests as the real reason reveals the vein of methodological pedantry which I have attributed to him. Plato, he says, is here writing as a natural philosopher and it would have been *inconveniens*, would have been a solecism, to say more about the daemons. Daemonology belongs to the higher discipline called *epoptica* (an *epoptes* was one who had been initiated into the mysteries).[2]

[1] CXCVIII, p. 240.   [2] CXXVII, p. 191.

A very brief reference to dreams in the original (45^e) leads to seven chapters on them in the commentary. These are of interest for two reasons. In the first place, they include[1] a translation of *Republic* 571^c, and thus hand on, ages before Freud, Plato's ur-Freudian doctrine of the dream as the expression of a submerged wish. Banquo knows about it.[2] In the second place, they throw light on a passage in Chaucer. Chalcidius lists the types of dream, and his list does not exactly agree with the better known classification of Macrobius. It includes, however, the *revelatio*, a type vouched for by *Hebraica philosophia*.[3] It will be remembered that Chaucer in the *Hous of Fame*, though otherwise reproducing the classification of Macrobius, adds one more type, the *revelacioun*. He doubtless derived it, though perhaps indirectly, from Chalcidius.

Astronomy in Chalcidius has not yet fully settled down in its medieval form. Like everyone else, he declares that the Earth is infinitesimally small by cosmic standards,[4] but the order of the planets is still open to dispute.[5] Nor are their names yet irrevocably fixed. He gives (here agreeing with the Aristotelian *De Mundo*) *Phaenon* as an alternative to Saturn, *Phaethon* to Jupiter, *Pyrois* to Mars, *Stilbon* to Mercury, and either *Lucifer* or *Hesperus* to Venus. He also holds that 'the diverse and multiple motion of the planets is the real source (*auctoritatem dedit*)[6] of all the effects that now come to pass'. All that

---

[1] CCLIII, p. 285. [2] *Macbeth*, II, i, 7.
[3] CCLVI, p. 289 [4] LIX, p. 127.
[5] LXXIII, p. 141. [6] LXXV, p. 143.

is suffered (*cunctae passiones*)[1] in this mutable world below
the Moon has its origin from them. But he is careful to
add that such influence upon us is not in any sense the
purpose for which they exist. It is a mere by-product.
They run the course appropriate to their beatitude, and
our contingent affairs imitate that felicity in such halting
fashion as they can. Thus, for Chalcidius, the geocentric
universe is not in the least anthropocentric. If we ask
why, nevertheless, the Earth is central, he has a very
unexpected answer. It is so placed in order that the
celestial dance may have a centre to revolve about—in
fact, as an aesthetic convenience for the celestial beings.
It is perhaps because his universe is already so well and
radiantly inhabited that Chalcidius, though he mentions[2]
the Pythagorean doctrine (which peopled the Moon and
other planets with mortals), is not interested in it.

Nothing will seem stranger to a modern than the
series of chapters which Chalcidius entitles 'On the
utility of Sight and Hearing'. The primary value of sight
is not, for him, its 'survival-value'. The important thing
is that sight begets philosophy. For 'no man would seek
God nor aspire to piety unless he had first seen the sky and
the stars'.[3] God gave men eyes in order that they might
observe 'the wheeling movements of mind and providence in the sky' and then, in the movements of their
own souls, try to imitate as nearly as they can that wisdom, serenity, and peace.[4] This is all genuine Plato (from
Timaeus 47[b]), though hardly the Plato we learn most of

---

[1] LXXVI, p. 144.   [2] CC, p. 241.
[3] CCLXIV, p. 296.   [4] CCLXV, p. 296.

at a modern university. Similarly, hearing exists principally for the sake of music. The native operations of the soul are related to the rhythms and modes. But this relationship fades in the soul because of her union with the body, and therefore the souls of most men are out of tune. The remedy for this is music; 'not that sort which delights the vulgar...but that divine music which never departs from understanding and reason'.[1]

Though Chalcidius had invented a reason for Plato's reticence on the subject of daemons, he does not follow his example. His account of them differs in some respects from that given by Apuleius. He denies the Pythagorean or Empedoclean belief that dead men become daemons;[2] all daemons are for him a distinct species, and he applies the name *daemons* to the aetherial as well as to the aerial creatures, the former being those whom 'the Hebrews call holy angels'.[3] But he is completely at one with Apuleius in affirming the Principle of Plenitude and that of the Triad. Aether and air, like Earth, must be populated 'lest any region be left void',[4] 'lest the perfection of the universe should anywhere go limping'.[5] And since there exist divine, immortal, celestial, and stellar creatures and also temporal, mortal, earthly, and passible creatures, 'it is inevitable that between these two there must exist some mean, to connect the extremes, as we see in harmony'.[6] We need not doubt that the voice which issued prohibitions to

[1] CCLXVII, p. 298. [2] CXXXVI, p. 198.
[3] CXXXII, p. 195. [4] CXXX, p. 193.
[5] CXXXVII, p. 199. [6] CXXXI, p. 194.

Socrates came from God; but we may be equally sure that it was not the voice of God itself. Between the purely intelligible God and the earthily corporeal Socrates there would be no unmediated *conciliatio*. God spoke to him through some 'mean', some intermediate being.[1] We may seem to be moving here in a world utterly alien to the Christian; but we shall find statements not unlike this of Chalcidius in authors whose Christianity has never been questioned.

So far Chalcidius is on common ground with Apuleius. He then proceeds to another application of the Triad. The cosmic Triad can be envisaged not only as a harmony but as a polity, a triad of sovereign, executive and subjects; the stellar powers command, the angelic beings execute, and the terrestrials obey.[2] Then, following the *Timaeus* (69^c–72^d) and the *Republic* (441^d–442^d), he finds the same triadic pattern repeated in the ideal state and in the human individual. In his imagined city Plato assigned the highest parts to his philosophical rulers who command. After them comes the warrior caste which carries out their orders. Finally, the common people obey. So in each man. The rational part lives in the body's citadel (*capitolium*), that is, the head. In the camp or barracks (*castra*) of the chest, warrior-like, the 'energy which resembles anger', that which makes a man high-spirited, has its station. Appetite, which corresponds to the common people, is located in the abdomen below them both.[3]

It will be seen how faithfully their triadic conception of

---

[1] CCLV, p. 288.   [2] CXXXII, p. 269.   [3] *Ibid.*

psychological health reflects either the Greek or the later medieval idea of the nurture proper to a freeman or a knight. Reason and appetite must not be left facing one another across a no-man's-land. A trained sentiment of honour or chivalry must provide the 'mean' that unites them and integrates the civilised man. But it is equally important for its cosmic implications. These were fully drawn out, centuries later, in the magnificent passage where Alanus ab Insulis compares the sum of things to a city. In the central castle, in the Empyrean, the Emperor sits enthroned. In the lower heavens live the angelic knighthood. We, on Earth, are 'outside the city wall'.[1] How, we ask, can the Empyrean be the centre when it is not only on, but outside, the circumference of the whole universe? Because, as Dante was to say more clearly than anyone else, the spatial order is the opposite of the spiritual, and the material cosmos mirrors, hence reverses, the reality, so that what is truly the rim seems to us the hub.

The exquisite touch which denies our species even the tragic dignity of being outcasts by making us merely sub-urban, was added by Alanus. In other respects he reproduces Chalcidius' outlook. We watch 'the spectacle of the celestial dance'[2] from its outskirts. Our highest privilege is to imitate it in such measure as we can. The Medieval Model is, if we may use the word, anthropo-peripheral. We are creatures of the Margin.

Chalcidius handed on more than the *Timaeus*. He

---

[1] *De Planctu Naturae, Prosa*, III, 108 *sq.* in Wright, *Anglo-Latin Satirical Poets*.　　　　[2] Chalcidius, LXV, p. 132.

quotes, sometimes at moderate length, from the *Crito*, *Epinomis*, *Laws*, *Parmenides*, *Phaedo*, *Phaedrus*, *Republic*, *Sophist*, and *Theaetetus*. He knows Aristotle but has little of the later reverence for him. Aristotle had passed over all save one of the species of dreams 'with his usual supercilious negligence' (*more quodam suo...fastidiosa incuria*).[1] He quotes and expands him, however, with more respect when arguing that matter, though not inherently evil, being the potentiality of all particular bodies, is doomed to (though logically distinct from) the privation (στέρησις, *carentia*) of Form.[2] That is why matter craves her perfecting or embellishment (*illustratio*) as the female desires the male.[3]

The influence of Chalcidius produces its richest results in the twelfth-century Latin poets associated with the school of Chartres, who in their turn helped to inspire Jean de Meung and Chaucer. The Lady Natura, from Statius and Claudian, and the cosmogony of Chalcidius, might be said to be the parents of Bernardus Silvester's *De Mundi Universitate*. Its feminine Noys (νοῦς, *Providentia*), so oddly introduced where we should expect the Second Person of the Christian Trinity, shows her lineage unmistakably: and perhaps owes her gender not so much to any Jungian archetype as to the gender of *Providentia* in Latin. In Chalcidius too we find the probable explanation of the mysterious garden called *Granusion*[4] which Bernard's Urania and Natura enter on descending to Earth. Chalcidius had distinguished not only aether

[1] CCL, p. 284.
[2] CCLXXXVI, pp. 316 *sq.* Cf. Aristotle, *Physics*, 192[a].
[3] Chalcidius, p. 317.   [4] II, ix, p. 52.

from air but also upper air from lower, the lower, which men can breathe, being a moist substance, *umecta substantia*, 'which the Greeks call *hygran usian*'.[1] Bernard knew no Greek, and the (to him meaningless) *hygranusian*, perhaps in a bad text, has become the proper name *Granusion*. In Bernard's successor, Alanus ab Insulis, we find an equally close linkage. In his *Anticlaudian*[2] we are told that the soul is fastened to the body *gumphis subtilibus*, 'with tiny little nails'. We may smile at the (almost 'metaphysical') quaintness of the image, which, if deliberate, would be quite characteristic of Alanus. In reality he is exactly following Chalcidius,[3] who is exactly following Plato,[4] and may not even know very clearly what a *gumphus* is. Such trifles deserve mention only as illustrations of the close discipleship that Chalcidius won from the poets of Chartres. The importance of that discipleship lies in the vigour, the gusto and sprightliness, of their response and the part it played in recommending certain images and attitudes to the vernacular authors.

B. MACROBIUS

Macrobius lived at the end of the fourth and the beginning of the fifth centuries. His religion also has been doubted, but there seems no solid reason for supposing that it was other than Paganism. He belonged, however, to a circle in which Christian and Pagan could freely mingle. The Christian Albinus and that great Pagan champion the elder Symmachus were among his friends. Of his two

---

[1] Chalcidius, CXXIX, p. 193.   [2] Wright, *op. cit.* VII, ii, 4, p. 384.
[3] CCIII, p. 243.   [4] *Timaeus*, 43[a].

works, the *Saturnalia*, a long, learned, urbane, and rambling conversation-piece, does not concern us. Our business is with his commentary[1] on the *Somnium Scipionis*. This, and the text which accompanied it, saved that part of Cicero's *Republic* for us. Nearly fifty manuscripts survive; it was a work of immense reputation and long-lasting influence.

On geography Macrobius repeats Cicero's doctrine of the five zones. It is reasonable to suppose that the Southern Temperate Zone is, like ours, inhabited, 'but we never have had, and shall never have, the possibility of discovering by whom'. Macrobius finds it still necessary (it would not have been in the Middle Ages) to remove a childish misunderstanding of what we call gravitation. There is no danger lest the inhabitants of the southern hemisphere should fall off into the nether sky; the Earth's surface is 'down' for them as it is for us (II, v). The Ocean covers most of the Torrid Zone; two great branches from it in the East, and two in the West, flow North and South, to meet at the Poles. From the meeting of their currents the tides result. The dry land thus falls into four main divisions. The great land-mass of Europe, Asia, and Africa is doubtless one of these four (II, ix). A diagrammatically simplified version of this lay-out survives in the later 'wheel-maps'. As we are cut off, in space, from the Antipodes, so we are almost cut off, in time, from most of the past. Nearly the whole human race has frequently been destroyed by great global

[1] Trans. W. H. Stahl, *Macrobius: On the Dream of Scipio* (Columbia, 1952).

catastrophes; nearly, for there has always been a remnant. Egypt has never been destroyed; that is why Egyptian records remount to an antiquity elsewhere unknown (II, x). The idea goes back to Plato's *Timaeus* (21ᵉ–23ᵇ) which in its turn may have been suggested by the delightful story in Herodotus (II, 143): Hecataeus the historian, visiting Egyptian Thebes, boasted that he was descended from a god in the sixteenth generation—which would take him safely back to a period before any continuous Greek records. Then the priests took him into a hall where stood the statues of those who had held the hereditary priesthood, and traced the line back, son to father, son to father; when they had reached the 145th generation they had still not come within sight of a god or even a demigod. This reflects the real difference between Greek and Egyptian history.

Thus, though civilisation in most parts of the Earth is always comparatively recent, the universe has always existed (II, x). If Macrobius describes its formation in terms which imply time, this must be taken merely as a convenience of discourse. Whatever was purest and most limpid (*liquidissimum*) rose to the highest place and was called aether. That which had less purity and some small degree of weight became air and sank to the second level. That which had still some fluidity but was gross (*corpulentum*) enough to offer tactual resistance, was gathered together into the stream of water. Finally, out of the whole tumult of matter all that was irreclaimable (*vastum*) was scraped off and cleansed from the (other) elements (*ex defaecatis abrasum elementis*), and sank down and settled at the lowest point, plunged in binding and unending cold (I, xxii). Earth is in fact the 'offscourings of creation', the cosmic dust-bin. This passage may also throw light on one in Milton. In *Paradise Lost*, VII, the Son has just marked out the spherical area of the Universe with His golden compasses (225). Then the spirit of God

> downward purg'd
> The black tartareous cold infernal dregs. (237)

Verity takes this to mean that He expelled them from the spherical area, purging them 'down' into chaos, which in Milton, for certain purposes, has an absolute up and down. But 'down' might equally well mean towards the centre of the cosmic sphere, and 'dregs' would exactly fit the conception of Macrobius.

To a modern reader what Macrobius has to say about dreams (I, iii) will seem a not very important item in his commentary; the Middle Ages must have thought differently, since it is clearly to this section that he owes the title *Ornicensis* or *Onocresius* which follows his name in some manuscripts and is there explained as *quasi somniorum iudex* or *somniorum interpres*: both words would be garbled transliterations of ὀνειροκρίτης. His scheme is derived from the *Oneirocritica* of Artemidorus (first century A.D.). According to it there are five species of dreams, three veridical, and two which have 'no divination' (*nihil divinationis*) in them. The veridical kinds are as follows:

(1) *Somnium* (ὄνειρος). This shows us truths veiled in an allegorical form. Pharaoh's dream of the fat and lean kine would be a specimen. Every allegorical dream-poem

in the Middle Ages records a feigned *somnium*. Nearly all dreams are assumed to be *somnia* by modern psychologists, and the *somnium* is the 'dreem' in Chaucer's *Hous of Fame*, I, 9.

(2) *Visio* (ὅραμα). This is a direct, literal pre-vision of the future. Mr Dunne's *Experiment with Time* is mainly about *visiones*. This type appears as 'avisioun' in Chaucer (*op. cit.* I, 7).

(3) *Oraculum* (χρηματισμός). In this one of the dreamer's parents or 'some other grave and venerable person' appears and openly declares the future or gives advice. Such dreams are Chaucer's 'oracles' (*op. cit.* I, 11). The useless kinds are:

(1) *Insomnium* (ἐνύπνιον). This merely repeats working preoccupations—'the carter dremeth how his cartes goon' as Chaucer says (*Parlement*, 102).

(2) *Visum* (φάντασμα). This occurs when, not yet fully asleep and believing ourselves to be still awake, we see shapes rushing towards us or flitting hither and thither. *Epialtes* or nightmare is included in this class. Chaucer's 'fantom' is clearly the *visum* (*Hous of Fame*, I, 11), and his 'sweven' is presumably an *insomnium*. This is more likely than the alternative equation ('dreem' for *visum* and 'sweven' for *somnium*) in view of the contempt with which Dame Pertelote speaks of 'swevenes' in B 4111–13; she was a well-educated bird and knew both physic and the *Distychs* of Dionysius Cato.

A dream may combine the characters of more than one species. Scipio's dream is an *oraculum* in so far as a venerable person appears in it to predict and warn; a *visio* in so far as it gives literal truths about the celestial regions; a *somnium*, in so far as its highest meaning, its *altitudo*, is concealed. To this *altitudo* we must now turn.

Cicero, as we have seen, devised a heaven for statesmen. He looks no higher than public life and the virtues which that life demands. Macrobius brings to the reading of Cicero a wholly different point of view—the mystical, ascetic, world-renouncing theology of neo-Platonism. The centre of interest for him lies in the purgation of the individual soul, the ascent 'of the alone to the Alone', and nothing could well be more foreign to the mind of Cicero.

This change of spiritual atmosphere meets us very early in his commentary. Cicero's feigned *somnium* could be attacked, as Plato's vision of Er had been attacked, on the ground that no species of fiction is becoming to a philosopher. Macrobius replies by distinguishing different kinds of *figmentum*: (1) where all is feigned as in a comedy by Menander. No philosopher would use this. (2) Where the reader's mind is stimulated to behold some form (or appearance) of virtues (or powers)—*ad quandam virtutum speciem*. This may be subdivided into (2A) and (2B). In (2A) the whole story is feigned, as in Aesop's fables; but in (2B) 'the argument is grounded in solid truth but that truth itself is exhibited by means of fictions'. The stories about the gods in Hesiod or Orpheus (which of course Macrobius interpreted allegorically) are examples. The knowledge of holy things is here hidden under 'a pious veil of figments'. This last is the only sort which philosophy admits. But note: it does not admit even this on all its themes. It will treat thus of the soul or of the aerial and aetherial beings or of 'the other gods'. But the licence to feign extends no further. Philosophy would never use this method when speaking 'of God the highest and first of all things, whom the Greeks call τἀγαθόν (the Good) and πρῶτον αἴτιον (the First Cause), or of Mind, whom the Greeks call νοῦς, which is the offspring of and procession from the Highest, wherein dwell the archetypal Forms of things which are called Ideas' (I, ii). We have here a chasm between the Divine and all merely creaturely beings (however exalted), a sheer transcendence, which earlier Paganism, and especially Roman Paganism, had never dreamed of. The word *gods* in this system is simply not the plural of *God*; there is a difference in kind, even an incommensurability, between them, as there is also between the 'holiness' of the 'holy things' (*sacra*) shadowed forth in Orpheus or Hesiod and that Holiness which Macrobius, though he does not use the word, so obviously feels when he thinks of the First Cause. Paganism here becomes, in the full sense, religious; mythology and philosophy have both been transmuted into theology.

The *God* and *Mind* mentioned in the last paragraph are of course the first two members (or persons? or moments?) of that neo-Platonic Trinity which is at once so like and so unlike the Christian. God *de se Mentem creavit*, created Mind out of Himself. A Christian would probably be ill-advised to give *creavit* a sense that could be opposed to 'begot'. The words 'out of Himself' discourage the Nicene distinction ('begotten not created') and *creare* in

Latin is freely used of sexual generation. This *Mens* is the *Noys* of Bernardus Silvestris. As soon as Macrobius begins to describe *Mens*, he reveals a profound difference between neo-Platonism and Christianity. 'In so far as *Mens* contemplates her parent she preserves the full likeness of her author; but when she looks back at things behind her, she creates out of herself *Anima*, Soul' (i, xiv). The Second Person of the Christian Trinity is the Creator, the provident wisdom and creative will of the Father in action. The idea that He became less one with, or turned away from, the Father by creating would be repugnant to Christian theology. In *Mens*, on the other hand, creation is almost a sort of infirmity. She becomes less like God by creating, declines into creation only because she turns her gaze away from her origin and looks back. The next step is the same. As long as *Anima* fixes her attention on *Mens* she puts on the nature of *Mens*; but gradually, as her contemplation withdraws, she sinks (*degenerat*), though herself incorporeal, to the making of bodies. That is how Nature comes into existence. Thus from the very beginning, where Christianity sees creation, neo-Platonism sees, if not exactly a Fall, yet a series of declensions, diminutions, almost of inconstancies. The universe seeps, as it were, into existence at those moments (for we can talk only in temporal language) when Mind is not perfectly 'waiting upon' God, nor Soul upon Mind. We must not, however, press this too far. Even on these terms the glory (*fulgor*) of God illumines the whole world 'as one face fills many mirrors placed in due order'. Dante uses this image in *Paradiso*, XXIX, 144–5.

All this, I suspect, would have interested Cicero very little; certainly Macrobius, thinking such thoughts, cannot be content with an ethic, and an eschatology, centred on civic life. Here, therefore, occurs one of those amazing *tours de force* to which syncretism is driven by its determination to find in all old texts what its own age accepts as Wisdom. Cicero, explaining his statesmen's heaven, had said that 'Nothing—nothing anyway that goes on on earth (*quod quidem in terris fiat*)—is more pleasing to God than those councils and communities of men bound together by law which we call commonwealths' (*Somnium*, xiii). What Cicero meant by his parenthetical reservation I am not sure; probably he was distinguishing earthly affairs from the motions of the heavenly bodies, which God would undoubtedly prize more highly. But Macrobius (I, viii) regards this saving clause as Cicero's way of leaving room for a whole system of ethics which Cicero might have strongly repudiated: a system which is religious, not secular; individual, not social; occupied not with the outer but with the inner life. He accepts the classical quaternion of virtues, Prudence, Temperance, Fortitude and Justice. But he adds that they all exist on four different levels and on each level their names have different meanings. On the lowest, or Political, level they mean what we should expect. The next level is the Purgatorial. Up there Prudence means 'to contemplate divine matters with contempt of the world and all that it contains'; Temperance, 'to renounce, so far as nature permits, all things that the body requires'; and Justice, to accept the practice of all the virtues as the only road to the good. Fortitude, on this level, is not so easily grasped. It enjoins 'that the soul be not terrified when, led by philosophy, she recedes in a manner from the body, and may feel no shudder at the height of the perfect ascent'. This is based on *Phaedo*, 81ᵃ⁻ᵈ. On the third level, which is that of souls already purified, Prudence means no longer to prefer divine things but to take no account at all of any others. Temperance means, not to deny, but wholly to forget, earthly desires. Fortitude means, not to conquer the passions but to be ignorant of their very existence; and Justice, 'to be so linked with that higher and divine Mind that one keeps an inviolable pact with her by imitation of her'. There remains the fourth level. Within *Mens* or νοῦς itself dwell the four Archetypal Virtues (*virtutes exemplares*), the transcendent Forms, whereof the four on the lower levels are shadows. Apparently it was to leave room for all this that Cicero wrote the five words *quod quidem in terris fiat*.

Like Cicero, Macrobius believes that the soul can return to heaven because she first came thence;[1] that the body is the soul's tomb;[2] that the soul is the man;[3] and that each single star is larger than the Earth.[4] Unlike most authorities, however, he denies that the stars produce terrestrial events, though they may by their relative positions enable us to predict them.

[1] I, ix.
[2] II, xii. This is an old Greek semi-pun on σῶμα and σῆμα.
[3] II, xii.   [4] I, xvi.

C. PSEUDO-DIONYSIUS

In the Middle Ages four books (*The Celestial Hierarchies, The Ecclesiastical Hierarchies, The Divine Names* and the *Mystical Theology*) were attributed to that Dionysius who was converted by hearing St Paul's address to the Areopagus.[1] This attribution was disproved in the sixteenth century. The real author is thought to have lived in Syria, and he must have written some time before 533, when his works were quoted at the Council of Constantinople. He was Latinised by John Scotus Eriugena who died about 870.

His writings are usually regarded as the main channel by which a certain kind of Theology entered the Western tradition. It is the 'negative Theology' of those who take in a more rigid sense, and emphasise more persistently than others, the incomprehensibility of God. It is already well rooted in Plato himself, as we see from *Republic* 509[b] and the Second Epistle[2] (312[e]–313[a]), and central in Plotinus. Its most striking representative in English is *The Cloud of Unknowing*. Some German Protestant Theology in our own time, and some Theistic Existentialism, has perhaps a remote affinity with it.

But this, though the most important thing about pseudo-Dionysius, is not the one that concerns us. It is by his angelology that he contributed to the Model, and we can therefore confine our attention to his *Celestial Hierarchies*.[3]

---

[1] Acts xvii. 34.   [2] Authorship disputed.

[3] *Sancti Dionysii...opera omnia...studio Petri Lanselii...Lutetiae Parisiorum* (MDCXV).

Our author differs from all earlier and some later authorities by declaring the angels to be pure minds (*mentes*), unembodied. In art, to be sure, they are represented as corporeal *pro captu nostro*, as a concession to our capacity (i). And such symbolism, he adds, is not degrading, 'for even matter, deriving its existence from the true Beauty, has in the fashion of all its parts some traces of beauty and worth' (ii). This statement, in a book which came to be so authoritative, may be taken as proof that educated people in the Middle Ages never believed the winged men who represent angels in painting and sculpture to be more than symbols.

It was pseudo-Dionysius whose arrangement of the angelic creatures into what Spenser calls their 'trinall triplicities', into three 'Hierarchies' containing three species each, was finally accepted by the Church.[1]

The first Hierarchy contains the three species, Seraphim, Cherubim, and Thrones. These are the creatures closest to God. They face Him ἀμέσως, *nullius interiectu*, with nothing between, encircling Him with their ceaseless dance. The names of Seraph and Throne are both associated by this author with ideas of heat or burning; a characteristic well known to the poets. Hence Chaucer's somnour had 'a fyr-reed cherubinnes face',[2] and it was not only for rhyme's sake that Pope wrote 'the rapt Seraph that adores and burns'.[3]

The second Hierarchy contains the κυριότητες or Dominations; the ἐξουσίαι (*Potestates*, *Potentates*, or

---

[1] *See* Dante, *Par.* XXVIII, 133-5.   [2] *C.T.* Prol. 624.
[3] *Essay on Man*, I, 278.

Powers); and the δυνάμεις or 'Virtues'. This does not mean moral excellences but rather 'efficacies', as when we speak about the 'virtues' of a magic ring or a medicinal herb.

The activity of both these Hierarchies is directed towards God; they stand, so to speak, with their faces to Him and their backs to us. In the third and lowest Hierarchy we at last find creatures who are concerned with Man. It contains Princedoms (or Principalities, or Princes); Archangels; and Angels. The word *angel* is thus both a generic name for all the nine species contained in the three Hierarchies, and also a specific name for the lowest—as *sailor* in English sometimes includes all seafaring persons and is sometimes confined only to those who berth forward.

Princedoms are the guardians and patrons of nations, so that Theology names Michael the Prince of the Jews (ix). The scriptural source of this is Dan. xii. 1. If Dryden had written his Arthuriad, these creatures would now be better known, for he intended to use them as his 'machines'.[1] They are Milton's 'Angels president in every province'[2] and Thomas Browne's 'provincial guardians'.[3] The two remaining species, Archangels and Angels, are the 'angels' of popular tradition, the beings that 'appear' to human individuals.

They are indeed the only superhuman beings that do so, for pseudo-Dionysius is as certain as Plato or Apuleius that God encounters Man only through a 'mean', and reads his own philosophy into scripture as freely as

---

[1] *Original...of Satire*, ed. W. P. Ker, vol. II, pp. 34 *sq.*
[2] *P.R.* I, 447.   [3] *Urn Burial*, v.

Chalcidius had read his into the *Timaeus*. He cannot deny that Theophanies, direct appearances of God Himself to patriarchs and prophets, *seem* to occur in the Old Testament. But he is quite sure that this never really happens. These visions were in reality mediated through celestial, but created, beings 'as though the order of the divine law laid it down that creatures of a lower order should be moved God-ward by those of a higher' (iv). That the order of the divine law does so enjoin is one of his key-conceptions. His God does nothing directly that can be done through an intermediary; perhaps prefers the longest possible chain of intermediaries; devolution or delegation, a finely graded descent of power and goodness, is the universal principle. The Divine splendour (*illustratio*) comes to us filtered, as it were, through the Hierarchies.

This explains why even a message of such cosmic moment as the Annunciation, even to so exalted a person as Mary, was brought by an angelic being, and even by a mere archangel, a member of the lowest species but one: 'angels were first shown the divine mystery and, afterwards, the grace of knowing it reached us through them' (iv). On this point Aquinas, centuries later, quotes pseudo-Dionysius and confirms him. The thing was done thus (for several reasons, but among them) 'that even in so great a matter (*in hoc etiam*) the system (or pattern, *ordinatio*) whereby divine things reach us through the mediation of angels might be unbroken'.[1]

By a *tour de force* comparable to that which Macrobius performed when he made Cicero into a good neo-

[1] *Summa Theol.* III[a], Qu. xxx, Art. 2.

Platonist, our author finds his principle confirmed in Isa. vi. 3. There the Seraphim are crying to one another 'Holy, Holy, Holy'. Why to one another rather than to the Lord? Obviously because each angel is incessantly handing on his knowledge of God to the angels next below him in rank. It is, of course, a transforming, not a merely speculative, knowledge. Each busily makes his colleagues (*collegas*) 'images of God, bright mirrors' (iii).

In pseudo-Dionysius the whole universe becomes a fugue of which the Triad (agent–mean–patient) is the 'subject'. The total angelic creation is a mean between God and Man, and that in two senses. It is a dynamic mean, as God's executive. But it is also a mean as a lens is a mean, for the celestial Hierarchies are revealed to us in order that the Ecclesiastical hierarchy on earth may imitate, as nearly as possible, 'their divine service and office' (i). And the second Hierarchy is doubtless a mean between the first and the third, and in each Hierarchy the central species is a mean, and in each individual angel, as in each individual man, there are ruling, and intermediate, and obedient faculties.

The spirit of this scheme, though not every detail, is strongly present in the Medieval Model. And if the reader will suspend his disbelief and exercise his imagination upon it even for a few minutes, I think he will become aware of the vast re-adjustment involved in a perceptive reading of the old poets. He will find his whole attitude to the universe inverted. In modern, that is, in evolutionary, thought Man stands at the top of a stair whose foot is lost in obscurity; in this, he stands at the bottom of a stair whose top is invisible with light. He will also understand that something besides individual genius (that, of course) helped to give Dante's angels their unrivalled majesty. Milton, aiming at that, missed the target. Classicism had come in between. His angels have too much anatomy and too much armour, are too much like the gods of Homer and Virgil, and (for that very reason) far less like the gods of Paganism in its highest religious development. After Milton total degradation sets in and we finally reach the purely consolatory, hence waterishly feminine, angels of nineteenth-century art.

D. BOETHIUS

Boethius (480–524) is, after Plotinus, the greatest author of the seminal period, and his *De Consolatione Philosophiae* was for centuries one of the most influential books ever written in Latin. It was translated into Old High German, Italian, Spanish, and Greek; into French by Jean de Meung; into English by Alfred, Chaucer, Elizabeth I, and others. Until about two hundred years ago it would, I think, have been hard to find an educated man in any European country who did not love it. To acquire a taste for it is almost to become naturalised in the Middle Ages.

Boethius, scholar and aristocrat, was a minister to Theodoric the Ostrogoth, the first barbarian king in Italy and an Arian by religion, though no persecutor. As always, the word 'barbarian' might mislead. Though Theodoric was illiterate, he had passed his youth in high Byzantine society. He was in some ways a better ruler than many Roman emperors had been. His reign in

Italy was not a sheer monstrosity as, say, the rule of Chaka or Dingaan in nineteenth-century England would have been. It was more as if a (popish) highland chieftain (who had acquired a little polish and a taste for claret in the French service) had reigned over the partly Protestant and partly sceptical England of Johnson and Lord Chesterfield. It is not, however, surprising that the Roman aristocracy were soon caught intriguing with the Eastern Emperor in the hope of delivering themselves from this alien. Boethius, whether justly or not, fell under suspicion. He was imprisoned at Pavia. Presently they twisted ropes round his head till his eyes dropped out and finished him off with a bludgeon.

Now Boethius was undoubtedly a Christian and even a theologian; his other works bear titles like *De Trinitate* and *De Fide Catholica*. But the 'philosophy' to which he turned for 'consolation' in the face of death contains few explicitly Christian elements and even its compatibility with Christian doctrine might be questioned.

Such a paradox has provoked many hypotheses. As:

(1) That his Christianity was superficial and failed him when brought to the test, so that he had to fall back on what neo-Platonism could do for him.

(2) That his Christianity was solid as a rock and his neo-Platonism a mere game with which he distracted himself in his dungeon—as other prisoners in like case have tamed a spider or a rat.

(3) That the theological essays were not really written by the same man.

None of these theories seems to me necessary.

Though the *De Consolatione* was certainly written after his fall, in exile and perhaps under arrest, I do not think it was written in a dungeon nor in daily expectation of the executioner. Once, indeed, he speaks of *terror*;[1] once he describes himself as doomed to 'death and proscription';[2] once Philosophia accuses him of 'fearing the bludgeon and the axe'.[3] But the general tone of the book does not match these momentary outbursts. It is not that of a prisoner awaiting death but that of a noble and a statesman lamenting his fall—exiled,[4] financially damaged,[5] parted from his beautiful library,[6] stripped of his official dignities, his name scandalously traduced.[7] This is no language of the condemned cell. And some of the 'consolations' which Philosophia addresses to him would be comically cruel mockeries to a man in that situation—as when she reminds him that the place which is exile to him is home to others,[8] or that many would regard as wealth even those remains of his property which he has managed to save.[9] The Consolation Boethius seeks is not for death but for ruin. When he wrote the book he may have known that his life was in some danger. I do not think he despaired of it. Indeed he complains at the outset that death cruelly neglects wretches who would gladly die.[10]

If we had asked Boethius why his book contained philosophical rather than religious consolations, I do not

---

[1] I *Met.* I, 5; p. 128 in the Stewart and Rand's text with I.P.'s translation (Loeb Library, 1908). [2] I *Pros.* IV, p. 152.
[3] II *Pros.* V, p. 202. [4] I *Pros.* III, p. 138.
[5] II *Pros.* I, p. 172. [6] I *Pros.* IV, p. 154. [7] *Ibid.*
[8] II *Pros.* IV, p. 192. [9] *Ibid.* [10] I *Met.* I, 15, p. 128.

doubt that he would have answered, 'But did you not read my title? I wrote philosophically, not religiously, because I had chosen the consolations of philosophy, not those of religion, as my subject. You might as well ask why a book on arithmetic does not use geometrical methods.' Aristotle had impressed on all who followed him the distinction between disciplines and the propriety of following in each its appropriate method.[1] We have seen this at work in Chalcidius; and Boethius draws our attention to it in his argument. He compliments Philosophia on having used 'inborn and domestical proofs', not 'reasons fetched from without'.[2] That is, he congratulates himself on having reached conclusions acceptable to Christianity from purely philosophical premises—as the rules of art demanded. When, on the other hand, she draws near the doctrines of Hell and Purgatory, he makes her check herself—'for it is not now our business to discuss such matters'.[3]

But why, we may ask, did a Christian author impose upon himself this limitation? Partly, no doubt, because he knew where his true talent lay. But we can suggest another, and probably less conscious, motive. The distinction between Christian and Pagan can hardly, at that moment, have been more vividly present to his emotions than that between Roman and barbarian; especially since the barbarian was also a heretic. Catholic Christendom and that high Pagan past to which he felt so deep a loyalty were united in his outlook by their

---

[1] Cf. *Eth. Nic.* 1094[b], cap. 3.   [2] III *Pros.* XII, p. 292.
[3] V *Pros.* IV, p. 328.

common contrast to Theodoric and his huge, fair-skinned, beer-drinking, boasting thanes. This was no time for stressing whatever divided him from Virgil, Seneca, Plato, and the old Republican heroes. He would have been robbed of half his comfort if he had chosen a theme which forced him to point out where the great ancient masters had been wrong; he preferred one that enabled him to feel how nearly they had been right, to think of them not as 'they' but as 'we'.

As a result, the specifically Christian passages in the book are few. The martyrs are clearly referred to.[1] In contradiction to the Platonic view that the Divine and the human cannot meet except through a *tertium quid*, prayer is a direct *commercium* between God and Man.[2] When Philosophia, speaking of Providence, uses the words 'strongly and sweetly', from Wisdom viii. 1 Boethius replies, 'I am delighted with your argument, but much more by the very language you use'.[3] But far more often Boethius is saying what Plato or the neo-Platonists would have confirmed. Man, by his reason, is a divine animal;[4] the soul is fetched from heaven,[5] and her ascent thither is a return.[6] In his account of creation[7] Boethius is much closer to the *Timaeus* than to Scripture.

Apart from its contributions to the Model *De Consolatione* had some formal influence. It belongs to the kind called *Satira Menippea* in which prose sections alternate with (shorter) sections in verse. From Boethius this

[1] II *Pros.* IV, p. 194.   [2] V *Pros.* III, p. 380.
[3] III *Pros.* XII, p. 290.   [4] II *Pros.* V, 200.
[5] III *Met.* VI, p. 249.   [6] III *Pros.* XII, p. 288.
[7] III *Met.* IX, p. 264.

descends to Bernardus and Alanus and even into Sanna-zaro's *Arcadia*. (I have often wondered that it has never been revived. One would have thought that a Landor, a Newman, or an Arnold might have turned it to good account.)

In Book I the appearance of Philosophia as a woman both old and young[1] is borrowed from Claudian's *Natura* in the *Consulship of Stilicho* (ii, 424 *sq.*). It will re-appear in the *Natura* of the French poem which Lydgate translated as *Reason and Sensuality* (line 334). She tells him, among other things, that we—we philosophers—must anticipate calumny, for it is our express purpose (*maxime propositum*) to displease the rabble.[2] This towering vaunt, this philosophic *panache* which goes beyond mere indifference to mud-flinging and actually courts it, is of Cynic origin. Milton's Christ is infected with it, when he des-cribes the common herd as people 'of whom to be dis-prais'd were no small praise' in *Paradise Regained* (iii, 54). But poor Boethius is not yet ready for so high a strain; he is as deaf to it as a donkey to the harp—an image Chaucer appropriated in *Troilus*, i, 730. Everyone is now slander-ing him, though in reality his conduct while in office had been of flawless purity. He adds with almost comic inconsistency—Boethius the author here ruthlessly expos-ing Boethius the natural man—that his virtue was all the more admirable because he practised it with no thought of being admired. For, he adds, virtue is tarnished if a man displays it so as to get credit for it.[3]

---

[1] I *Pros.* i, p. 130. [2] I *Pros.* iii, p. 140.
[3] I *Pros.* iv, p. 150.

This modest maxim cuts right across the ideals of the Dark Ages and of the Renaissance. Roland unashamedly desires *los* as Beowulf desires *dom* or the heroes in French tragedy desire *la gloire*. It was often discussed in the later Middle Ages. Alanus knows it but agrees with it only up to a point. The good man should not make fame his object, but to reject it altogether is too austere (*Anticlaudian*, VII, iv, 26). Gower, on the other hand, applies it in its full rigour, even to knightly deeds,

> In armes lith non avantance
> To him that thenkth his name avance
> And be renomed of his dede.[1]

> (*Confessio Amantis*, I, 2651.)

Boethius then passionately demands an explanation of the contrast between the regularity with which God governs the rest of Nature and the irregularity He permits in human affairs.[2] This is made a central theme of Nature's 'complaint' in Alanus and of her 'confession' in Jean de Meung. Later still Milton is recalling, and no doubt expects us to recognise that he is recalling, this place from Boethius in one of the choruses of *Samson*, (667 *sq.*). The whole concept will seem less remote to some modern readers if they relate it to the Existentialist position that Man is a *passion inutile* and compares very unfavourably with the irrational or even the inorganic world.

With Book II we embark on that great apologia for Fortune which impressed her figure so firmly on the imagination of succeeding ages. Comments on good and

[1] Cf. *Vox Clamantis*, v, 17.   [2] Boethius, I *Met.* v, pp. 154 *sq.*

bad luck and their obvious failure to correspond with good and ill desert may be expected in any period; but the medieval allusions to Fortune and her wheel are exceptional in their frequency and seriousness. The grandeur which this image takes on in the *Inferno* (VII, 73 *sq.*) is a reminder how entirely it depends on individual genius whether a *locus communis* shall or shall not be what we call 'commonplace'. And this, like a thousand inferior passages, is part of the Boethian legacy. No one who had read of *Fortuna* as he treats her could forget her for long. His work, here Stoical and Christian alike, in full harmony with the Book of Job and with certain Dominical sayings,[1] is one of the most vigorous defences ever written against the view, common to vulgar Pagans and vulgar Christians alike, which 'comforts cruel men' by interpreting variations of human prosperity as divine rewards and punishments, or at least wishing that they were. It is an enemy hard to kill; latent in what has been called 'the Whig interpretation of history' and rampant in the historical philosophy of Carlyle.

At every point in this discussion we meet 'old friends'— that is, images and phrases which first became our friends when they had grown very much older.

Thus from Book II: 'The most miserable misfortune is to have been happy once.'[2] Dante's *nessun maggior dolore* (*Inferno*, V, 121) and Tennyson's 'sorrow's crown of sorrows' leap to mind. 'Nothing is miserable unless you think it so.'[3] We remember Chaucer's 'no man is wreched

---

[1] Luke xiii. 4; John ix. 13. [2] II *Pros.* IV, p. 188.
[3] II *Pros.* IV, p. 192.

but himself it wene' in the *Ballade of Fortune* and Hamlet's
'There is nothing either good or bad but thinking makes
it so'. We are told that we cannot lose external goods
because we never really had them. The beauty of fields or
gems is a real good, but it is theirs, not ours; the beauty of
clothes is either theirs (the richness of the stuff) or the skill
of the tailor—nothing will make it ours.[1] The idea will
turn up again unexpectedly in *Joseph Andrewes* (III, 6).
Soon after this we hear the praises of the *prior aetas*,[2] the
primeval innocence pictured by the Stoics. Readers of
Milton will here notice the *pretiosa pericula* which became
his 'precious bane'. From this *prior aetas* came both the
'Former Age' of Chaucer's ballade and 'the old age'
mentioned by Orsino (*Twelfth Night*, II, iv, 46). We are
told that nothing so much beguiles those who have some
natural excellence but are not yet perfected in virtue as
the desire for fame. It is a maxim from the *Agricola* of
Tacitus; it will later blossom into Milton's line about
'that last infirmity of noble mind'.

Philosophia proceeds to mortify this desire, as Africanus
had done in the *Somnium*, by pointing out how provincial
all earthly fame is since this globe, by cosmic standards, is
admittedly to be regarded as a mathematical point—
puncti habere rationem.[3] But Boethius deepens this stock
argument by stressing the diversity of moral standards
even within this tiny area. What is fame in one nation can
be infamy in another.[4] And anyway how short-lived all
reputations are ! Books, like their author, are mortal. No

[1] II *Pros.* v, pp. 198–200.   [2] II *Met.* v.
[3] II *Pros.* VII, p. 212.   [4] *Ibid.* p. 214.

one now knows where the bones of Fabricius lie.[1] (Here, for the benefit of his English readers, Alfred happily substituted 'the bones of Weland'.)

Adversity has the merit of opening our eyes by showing which of our friends are true and which are feigned.[2] Combine this with Vincent of Beauvais' statement that hyena's gall restores the sight (*Speculum Naturale*, XIX, 62), and you have the key to Chaucer's cryptic line 'Thee nedeth nat the gall of noon hyene' (*Fortune*, 35).

From Book III: All men know that the true good is Happiness, and all men seek it, but, for the most part, by wrong routes—like a drunk man who knows he has a house but can't find his way home.[3] Chaucer reproduces the simile in the *Knight's Tale* (A 1261 *sq.*).

Yet even the false routes, such as wealth or glory, show that men have some inkling of the truth; for the true good is glorious like fame and, like wealth, self-sufficient. So strong is the bent of nature that we thus struggle towards our native place, as the caged bird struggles to return to the woods. Chaucer borrows this image for his *Squire's Tale* (F 621 *sq.*).

One of the false images of the good is Nobility. But Nobility is only the fame (and we have already exploded fame) of our ancestors' virtue, which was a good of theirs, not ours.[4] This doctrine had a flourishing progeny in the Middle Ages, and became a popular subject for school debates. It underlies Dante's *canzone* at the opening of *Convivio*, IV, and the other place in *De Monarchia* (II, 3).

---

[1] II *Met.* VII, p. 218. [2] II *Pros.* VIII, p. 220.
[3] III *Pros.* II, p. 230. [4] III *Pros.* VI, p. 248.

The *Roman de la Rose* (18,615 *sq.*) goes beyond Boethius and boldly equates *gentilesse* with virtue. The English version at this point (2185–202) further expands its French original. *The Wife of Bath* reproduces Boethius more exactly (D 1154). Gower, like the *Roman*, identifies nobility with 'vertu set in the corage' (IV, 2261 *sq.*). One may be forgiven a smile when a (not otherwise very ignorant) author finds in this passage a proof that Gower expresses the feelings of the middle class which in his day was (as usual) 'rising into new importance'.

The argument now climbs to the position that the whole and perfect good, of which we usually chase only fragments or shadows, is God. In the course of proving this—though it needed no new proof either for Platonists or Christians—Boethius slips in, as axiomatic, the remark that all perfect things are prior to all imperfect things.[1] It was common ground to nearly all ancient and medieval thinkers except the Epicureans.[2] I have already[3] stressed the radical difference which this involves between their thought and the developmental or evolutionary concepts of our own period—a difference which perhaps leaves no area and no level of consciousness unaffected.

Those who have once risen to contemplate 'the admirable circle of the divine simplicity'[4] must be careful not to look back again to worldly objects. The moral is enforced by the story of Orpheus and his fatal backward glance at Eurydice, and this telling of that story was as widely influential as Virgil's. It is also of great structural import-

[1] III *Pros.* X, p. 268.　　[2] See Lucretius, v.
[3] See above, p. 74.　　[4] III *Pros.* XII, p. 292.

ance in the *De Consolatione*, for Boethius himself, when Philosophia visited him in Book I, was indulging in just such a retrospection. Here, too, he reaches his highest point as a poet in the famous lines

> Orpheus Eurydicen suam
> Vidit, perdidit, occidit.[1]

From Book IV: The doctrine of divine Providence, Boethius complains, rather aggravates than solves the real problem: why is justice—certainly 'poetic justice'—so unapparent in the course of events? Philosophia makes two replies.

(1) It is all justice. The good are always rewarded and the wicked always punished, by the mere fact of being what they are. Evil power and evil performance are the punishment of evil will,[2] and it will be infinite since the soul is immortal (as philosophy, no less than Theology, asserts). The passage looks back to Virgil's hell whose inhabitants *ausi omnes immane nefas ausoque potiti*, 'all purposed dreadful deeds *and got their way*' (*Aeneid*, VI, 624). It looks forward to Milton who says of the wiser Pagans that 'to banish forever into a local hell...they thought not a punishment so proper and proportionate for God to inflict as to punish sin with sin' (*Doctrine and Discipline*, II, 3). And yet, pleads Boethius, it is very strange to see the wicked flourishing and the virtuous afflicted. Why, yes, replies Philosophia; everything is strange until you know the cause.[3] Compare the *Squire's Tale* (F 258).

[1] III *Met.* XII, p. 296 (One backward glance sufficed to see, To lose, to kill, Eurydice).
[2] IV *Pros.* IV, pp. 322, 324.　　[3] IV *Pros.* V and *Met.* V, pp. 334-8.

(2) That which 'in the citadel of the divine simplicity' is Providence, when seen from below, mirrored in the multiplicity of time and space, is Destiny.[1] And as in a wheel the nearer we get to the centre the less motion we find, so every finite being, in proportion as he comes nearer to participating in the Divine (unmoving) Nature, becomes less subject to Destiny, which is merely a moving image of eternal Providence. That Providence is wholly good. We say that the wicked flourish and the innocent suffer. But we do not know who are the wicked and who are the innocent; still less what either need. All luck, seen from the centre, is good and medicinal. The sort we call 'bad' exercises good men and curbs bad ones—if they will take it so. Thus, if only you are near the hub, if you participate in Providence more and suffer Destiny less, 'it lies in your own hands to make your fortune what you please'.[2] Or, as Spenser turns this passage, 'each unto himself his life may fortunize' (*F.Q.* VI, ix, 30).

The noblest descendant of this passage, however, is not in words. At Rome in Santa Maria del Popolo the cupola above Chigi's tomb sets the whole Boethian image of the wheel and the hub, of Destiny and Providence, before our eyes. On the utmost circumference the planets, the dispensers of fate, are depicted. On a smaller circle, within and above them, are the Intelligences that move them. At the centre, with hands upraised in guidance, sits the Unmoved Mover.[3]

[1] IV *Pros.* VI, p. 380.   [2] IV *Pros.* VII, p. 360.
[3] J. Seznec, *The Survival of the Pagan Gods*, trans. B. F. Sessions (1953), p. 80.

In the fifth and last book the argument is closer, and succeeding generations were unable to pluck out of it many isolated plums. But this does not mean that it proved less influential. It underlies every later treatment of the problem of freedom.

The conclusion of the previous book has left us with a new difficulty. If, as its doctrine of Providence implies, God sees all things that are, were, or will be, *uno mentis in ictu*,[1] in a single act of mind, and thus foreknows my actions, how am I free to act otherwise than He has foreseen? Philosophia will not put Boethius off with the shift that Milton is reduced to in *Paradise Lost* (III, 117), that, though God foreknows, His foreknowledge does not cause, my act. For the question never was whether foreknowledge necessitates the act but whether it is not evidence that the act must have been necessary.

Can there, then, be foreknowledge of the indeterminate? In a sense, yes. The character of knowledge depends not on the nature of the object known but on that of the knowing faculty. Thus in ourselves sensation, imagination, and *ratio* all in their several ways 'know' man. Sensation knows him as a corporeal shape; imagination, as a shape without matter; *ratio*, as a concept, a species. None of these faculties by itself gives us the least hint of the mode of knowledge enjoyed by its superior.[2] But above *ratio* or reason there is a higher faculty, *intelligentia* or understanding.[3] (Long afterwards Coleridge reversed this by making reason the higher and understanding the lower. I postpone further considera-

[1] V *Met.* II, p. 372.   [2] V *Pros.* V, p. 394.   [3] *Ibid.*

tion of the medieval terminology till a later section.) And Reason cannot conceive the future being known except as it would have to be known, if at all, by her; that is, as determinate. But it is just possible even for us to climb up to the intelligential level and get a glimpse of the knowledge which does not involve determinism.

Eternity is quite distinct from perpetuity, from mere endless continuance in time. Perpetuity is only the attainment of an endless series of moments, each lost as soon as it is attained. Eternity is the actual and timeless fruition of illimitable life.[1] Time, even endless time, is only an image, almost a parody, of that plenitude; a hopeless attempt to compensate for the transitoriness of its 'presents' by infinitely multiplying them. That is why Shakespeare's Lucrece calls it 'thou ceaseless lackey to eternity' (*Rape*, 967). And God is eternal, not perpetual. Strictly speaking, He never *fore*sees; He simply sees. Your 'future' is only an area, and only for us a special area, of His infinite Now. He sees (not remembers) your yesterday's acts because yesterday is still 'there' for Him; he sees (not foresees) your tomorrow's acts because He is already in tomorrow. As a human spectator, by watching my present act, does not at all infringe its freedom, so I am none the less free to act as I choose in the future because God, in that future (His present) watches me acting.[2]

I have so ruthlessly condensed an argument of such importance, both historical and intrinsic, that the wise reader will go for it to the original. I cannot help thinking

[1] V *Pros.* VI, p. 400.   [2] *Ibid.* pp. 402–10.

that Boethius has here expounded a Platonic conception more luminously than Plato ever did himself.

The work ends with Philosophia thus speaking; there is no return to Boethius and his situation, any more than to Christopher Sly at the end of *The Taming of the Shrew*. This I believe to be a stroke of calculated and wholly successful art. We are made to feel as if we had seen a heap of common materials so completely burnt up that there remains neither ash nor smoke nor even flame, only a quivering of invisible heat.

Gibbon has expressed in cadences of habitual beauty his contempt for the impotence of such 'philosophy' to subdue the feelings of the human heart. But no one ever said it would have subdued Gibbon's. It sounds as if it had done something for Boethius. It is historically certain that for more than a thousand years many minds, not contemptible, found it nourishing.

Before closing this chapter it will be convenient to mention two authors who are later in time and very much inferior in rank. They are not, like those whom I have been describing, contributors to the Model, but they sometimes supply the handiest evidence as to what it was. Both are encyclopaedists.

Isidore, Bishop of Seville from 600 to 636, wrote the *Etymologiae*. As the title implies his ostensible subject was language, but the frontier between explaining the meaning of words and describing the nature of things is easily violated. He makes hardly any effort to keep on the linguistic side of it, and his book thus becomes an encyclopaedia. It is a work of very mediocre intelligence, but often gives us scraps of information we cannot easily run to ground in better authors. It also has the enormous advantage of being accessible in a good modern edition.[1]

The same, unhappily, is not true of Vincent of Beauvais (*ob.* 1264). His huge *Speculum Majus* is divided into the *Speculum Naturale*, the *Speculum Doctrinale*, and the *Speculum Historiale*. We might expect that the 'Doctrinal Mirror' was concerned with Theology. Actually, it deals with morals, arts, and trades.

[1] Ed. W. M. Lindsay, 2 vols. (1910).

CHAPTER V

THE HEAVENS

Man, walke at large out of thi prisoun.
HOCCLEVE

A. THE PARTS OF THE UNIVERSE

The fundamental concept of modern science is, or was till very recently, that of natural 'laws', and every event was described as happening in 'obedience' to them. In medieval science the fundamental concept was that of certain sympathies, antipathies, and strivings inherent in matter itself. Everything has its right place, its home, the region that suits it, and, if not forcibly restrained, moves thither by a sort of homing instinct:[1]

> Every kindly thing that is
> Hath a kindly stede ther he
> May best in hit conserved be;
> Unto which place every thing
> Through his kindly enclyning
> Moveth for to come to.
>
> (Chaucer, *Hous of Fame*, II, 730 *sq.*)

Thus, while every falling body for us illustrates the 'law' of gravitation, for them it illustrated the 'kindly enclyning' of terrestrial bodies to their 'kindly stede' the Earth, the centre of the Mundus, for

> To that centre drawe
> Desireth every worldes thing.
>
> (Gower, *Confessio*, VII, 234.)

[1] Cf. Dante, *Par.* I, 109 *sq.*

Such was the normal language in the Middle Ages, and later. 'The see desyreth naturely to folwen' the Moon, says Chaucer (*Franklin's Tale*, F 1052). 'The iron', says Bacon, 'in particular sympathy moveth to the lodestone' (*Advancement*).[1]

The question at once arises whether medieval thinkers really believed that what we now call inanimate objects were sentient and purposive. The answer in general is undoubtedly no. I say 'in general', because they attributed life and even intelligence to one privileged class of objects (the stars) which we hold to be inorganic. But full-blown Panpsychism, the doctrine of universal sentience, was not (to the best of my knowledge) held by anyone before Campanella (1568–1639), and never made many converts. On the common medieval view there were four grades of terrestrial reality: mere existence (as in stones), existence with growth (as in vegetables), existence and growth with sensation (as in beasts), and all these with reason (as in men).[2] Stones, by definition, could not literally strive or desire.

If we could ask the medieval scientist 'Why, then, do you talk as if they did,' he might (for he was always a dialectician) retort with the counter-question, 'But do you intend your language about *laws* and *obedience* any more literally than I intend mine about *kindly enclyning*? Do you really believe that a falling stone is aware of a directive issued to it by some legislator and feels either a moral or a prudential obligation to conform?' We should

---

[1] Everyman edn., p. 156.
[2] Gregory, *Moralia*, VI, 16; Gower, *Confessio*, Prol. 945 *sq.*

then have to admit that both ways of expressing the facts are metaphorical. The odd thing is that ours is the more anthropomorphic of the two. To talk as if inanimate bodies had a homing instinct is to bring them no nearer to us than the pigeons; to talk as if they could 'obey laws' is to treat them like men and even like citizens.

But though neither statement can be taken literally, it does not follow that it makes no difference which is used. On the imaginative and emotional level it makes a great difference whether, with the medievals, we project upon the universe our strivings and desires, or with the moderns, our police-system and our traffic regulations. The old language continually suggests a sort of continuity between merely physical events and our most spiritual aspirations. If (in whatever sense) the soul comes from heaven, our appetite for beatitude is itself an instance of 'kindly enclyning' for the 'kindly stede'. Hence in *The King's Quair* (st. 173)

> O wery gost ay flickering to and fro
> That never art in quiet nor in rest
> Til thou com to that place that thou cam fro
> Which is thy first and very proper nest.[1]

The ultimately sympathetic and antipathetic properties in matter are the Four Contraries. Chaucer in one place enumerates six: 'hoot, cold, hevy, light, moist, and dreye' (*Parlement*, 379). But the usual list gives four: 'hot, cold,

---

[1] The passage in Chaucer's *Troilus*, IV, 302, is not, in the simplest sense, the 'source' of this. Chaucer had twisted the idea into an erotic conceit, but King James untwists Chaucer back into complete seriousness. Both poets knew clearly what they were doing.

moist and dry', as in *Paradise Lost*, II, 898. We meet them in Milton's Chaos thus raw because Chaos is not the universe but only its raw material. In the Mundus which God built out of that raw material we find them only in combination. They combine to form the four elements. The union of hot and dry becomes fire; that of hot and moist, air; of cold and moist, water; of cold and dry, earth. (In the human body they combine with a different result, as we shall see later.)[1] There is also a Fifth Element or Quintessence, the aether; but that is found only above the Moon and we mortals have no experience of it.

In the sublunary world—Nature in the strict sense—the four elements have all sorted themselves out into their 'kindly stedes'. Earth, the heaviest, has gathered itself together at the centre. On it lies the lighter water; above that, the still lighter air. Fire, the lightest of all, whenever it was free, has flown up to the circumference of Nature and forms a sphere just below the orbit of the Moon. Hence Spenser's Titaness in her ascent passes first 'the region of the ayre', then 'the fire', before reaching 'the circle of the Moone' (*F.Q.* VII, vi, 7, 8), and in Donne the soul of Elizabeth Drury is travelling from air to Moon so quickly that she does not know whether she went through the sphere of fire or not (*Second Anniversary*, 191–4). When Don Quixote and Sancho believed they had reached this stage in their imaginary ascent, the knight was very afraid they would be burnt (II, xli). The reason why flames always move upward is that the fire in them is seeking its 'kindly stede'. But flames are impure fire, and

[1] See below, p. 170.

it is only their impurity that makes them visible. The 'elemental fire' which forms a sphere just below the Moon is pure, unadulterated fire; hence invisible and completely transparent. It was this 'element of fire' that was 'quite put out' by 'new Philosophy'. That was part of Donne's reason for making Elizabeth Drury pass too quickly to solve the vexed question.

The architecture of the Ptolemaic universe is now so generally known that I will deal with it as briefly as possible. The central (and spherical) Earth is surrounded by a series of hollow and transparent globes, one above the other, and each of course larger than the one below. These are the 'spheres', 'heavens', or (sometimes) 'elements'. Fixed in each of the first seven spheres is one luminous body. Starting from Earth, the order is the Moon, Mercury, Venus, the Sun, Mars, Jupiter and Saturn; the 'seven planets'. Beyond the sphere of Saturn is the *Stellatum*, to which belong all those stars that we still call 'fixed' because their positions relative to one another are, unlike those of the planets, invariable. Beyond the *Stellatum* there is a sphere called the First Movable or *Primum Mobile*. This, since it carries no luminous body, gives no evidence of itself to our senses; its existence was inferred to account for the motions of all the others.

And beyond the *Primum Mobile* what? The answer to this unavoidable question had been given, in its first form, by Aristotle. 'Outside the heaven there is neither place nor void nor time. Hence whatever is there is of such a kind as not to occupy space, nor does time affect it.'[1] The timidity, the hushed voice, is characteristic of the best Paganism. Adopted into Christianity, the doctrine speaks loud and jubilant. What is in one sense 'outside the heaven' is now, in another sense, 'the very Heaven', *caelum ipsum*, and full of God, as Bernardus says.[2] So when Dante passes that last frontier he is told, 'We have got outside the largest corporeal thing (*del maggior corpo*) into that Heaven which is pure light, intellectual light, full of love' (*Paradiso*, XXX, 38). In other words, as we shall see more clearly later on, at this frontier the whole spatial way of thinking breaks down. There can be, in the ordinary spatial sense, no 'end' to a three-dimensional space. The end of space is the end of spatiality. The light beyond the material universe is intellectual light.

The dimensions of the medieval universe are not, even now, so generally realised as its structure; within my own lifetime a distinguished scientist has helped to disseminate error.[3] The reader of this book will already know that Earth was, by cosmic standards, a point—it had no appreciable magnitude. The stars, as the *Somnium Scipionis* had taught, were larger than it. Isidore in the sixth century knows that the Sun is larger, and the Moon smaller than the Earth (*Etymologies*, III, xlvii–xlviii), Maimonides in the twelfth maintains that every star is ninety times as big, Roger Bacon in the thirteenth simply that the least star is 'bigger' than she.[4] As to estimates of distance, we are fortunate in having the testimony of a thoroughly

[1] *De Caelo*, 279ª. [2] *De Mundi Universitate*, II Pros. VII, p. 48.
[3] J. B. S. Haldane, *Possible Worlds* (1930), p. 7.
[4] Lovejoy, *op. cit.* p. 100.

popular work, the *South English Legendary*: better evidence than any learned production could be for the Model as it existed in the imagination of ordinary people. We are there told that if a man could travel upwards at the rate of 'forty mile and yet som del mo' a day, he still would not have reached the *Stellatum* ('the highest heven that ye alday seeth') in 8000 years.[1]

These facts are in themselves curiosities of mediocre interest. They become valuable only in so far as they enable us to enter more fully into the consciousness of our ancestors by realising how such a universe must have affected those who believed in it. The recipe for such realisation is not the study of books. You must go out on a starry night and walk about for half an hour trying to see the sky in terms of the old cosmology. Remember that you now have an absolute Up and Down. The Earth is really the centre, really the lowest place; movement to it from whatever direction is downward movement. As a modern, you located the stars at a great distance. For distance you must now substitute that very special, and far less abstract, sort of distance which we call height; height, which speaks immediately to our muscles and nerves. The Medieval Model is vertiginous. And the fact that the height of the stars in the medieval astronomy is very small compared with their distance in the modern, will turn out not to have the kind of importance you antici-. pated. For thought and imagination, ten million miles and a thousand million are much the same. Both can be conceived (that is, we can do sums with both) and neither

[1] Ed. C. d'Evelyn, A. J. Mill (E.E.T.S., 1956), vol. II, p. 418.

can be imagined; and the more imagination we have the better we shall know this. The really important difference is that the medieval universe, while unimaginably large, was also unambiguously finite. And one unexpected result of this is to make the smallness of Earth more vividly felt. In our universe she is small, no doubt; but so are the galaxies, so is everything—and so what? But in theirs there was an absolute standard of comparison. The furthest sphere, Dante's *maggior corpo* is, quite simply and finally, the largest object in existence. The word 'small' as applied to Earth thus takes on a far more absolute significance. Again, because the medieval universe is finite, it has a shape, the perfect spherical shape, containing within itself an ordered variety. Hence to look out on the night sky with modern eyes is like looking out over a sea that fades away into mist, or looking about one in a trackless forest—trees forever and no horizon. To look up at the towering medieval universe is much more like looking at a great building. The 'space' of modern astronomy may arouse terror, or bewilderment or vague reverie; the spheres of the old present us with an object in which the mind can rest, overwhelming in its greatness but satisfying in its harmony. That is the sense in which our universe is romantic, and theirs was classical.

This explains why all sense of the pathless, the baffling, and the utterly alien—all agoraphobia—is so markedly absent from medieval poetry when it leads us, as so often, into the sky. Dante, whose theme might have been expected to invite it, never strikes that note. The meanest modern writer of science-fiction can, in that department, do more for you than he. Pascal's terror at *le silence éternel de ces espaces infinis* never entered his mind. He is like a man being conducted through an immense cathedral, not like one lost in a shoreless sea. The modern feeling, I suspect, first appears in Bruno. With Milton it enters English poetry, when he sees the Moon 'riding'

> Like one that had bin led astray
> Through the Heav'ns wide pathless way.

Later, in *Paradise Lost*, he invented a most ingenious device for retaining the old glories of the builded and finite universe yet also expressing the new consciousness of space. He enclosed his cosmos in a spherical envelope within which all could be light and order, and hung it from the floor of Heaven. Outside that he had Chaos, the 'infinite Abyss' (II, 405), the 'unessential Night' (438), where 'length, breadth and highth And time and place are lost' (891–2). He is perhaps the first writer to use the noun *space* in its fully modern sense—'space may produce new worlds '(I, 650).

It must, however, be admitted that while the moral and emotional consequences of the cosmic dimensions were emphasised, the visual consequences were sometimes ignored. Dante in the *Paradiso* (XXVII, 81–3) looks down from the sphere of the Fixed Stars and sees the northern hemisphere extended from Cadiz to Asia. But according to the Model the whole Earth could hardly be visible from that altitude, and to talk of seeing any markings on its surface is ridiculous. Chaucer in the *Hous of Fame* is lower by unimaginable distances than Dante, for he is still below the Moon in the air. But even so, it is extremely unlikely that he could have made out ships and even, though *unethes* (with difficulty), 'bestes' (II, 846–903).

The impossibility, under the supposed conditions, of such visual experiences is obvious to us because we have grown up from childhood under the influence of pictures that aimed at the maximum of illusion and strictly observed the laws of perspective. We are mistaken if we suppose that mere commonsense, without any such training, will enable men to see an imaginary scene, or even to see the world they are living in, as we all see it today.[1] Medieval art was deficient in perspective, and poetry followed suit. Nature, for Chaucer, is all foreground; we never get a landscape. And neither poets nor artists were much interested in the strict illusionism of later periods. The relative size of objects in the visible arts is determined more by the emphasis the artist wishes to lay upon them than by their sizes in the real world or by their distance. Whatever details we are meant to see will be shown whether they would really be visible or not. I believe Dante would have been quite capable of knowing that he could not have seen Asia and Cadiz from the *stellatum* and nevertheless putting them in. Centuries later Milton makes Raphael look down from the gate of Heaven, that is, from a point outside the whole sidereal universe—'distance inexpressible By Numbers that have name' (VIII, 113)—and see not only Earth, not only continents on Earth, not only Eden, but cedar trees (V, 257–61).

Of the medieval and even the Elizabethan imagination

[1] See E. H. Gombrich, *Art and Illusion* (1960).

in general (though not, as it happens, of Dante's) we may say that in dealing with even foreground objects, it is vivid as regards colour and action, but seldom works consistently to scale. We meet giants and dwarfs, but we never really discover their exact size. *Gulliver* was a great novelty.[1]

B. THEIR OPERATIONS

So far our picture of the universe is static; we must now set it in motion.

All power, movement, and efficacy descend from God to the *Primum Mobile* and cause it to rotate; the exact kind of causality involved will be considered later. The rotation of the *Primum Mobile* causes that of the *Stellatum*, which causes that of the sphere of Saturn, and so on, down to the last moving sphere, that of the Moon. But there is a further complexity. The *Primum Mobile* revolves from east to west, completing its circle every twenty-four hours. The lower spheres have (by 'kindly enclyning') a far slower revolution from west to east, which takes 36,000 years to complete. But the daily impulse of the *Primum Mobile* forces them daily back, as with its wash or current, so that their actual movement is westward but at a speed retarded by their struggle to move in the opposite direction. Hence Chaucer's apostrophe:

> O firste moeving cruel firmament
> With thy diurnal sweigh that crowdest ay
> And hurlest al from Est til Occident
> That naturelly wolde holde another way.
>
> > (*Canterbury Tales*, B 295 *sq.*)

[1] See below, pp. 113–16.

The reader will no doubt understand that this was no arbitrary fancy, but just such another 'tool' as the hypothesis of Copernicus; an intellectual construction devised to accommodate the phenomena observed. We have recently been reminded[1] how much mathematics, and how good, went to the building of the Model.

Besides movement, the spheres transmit (to the Earth) what are called Influences—the subject-matter of Astrology. Astrology is not specifically medieval. The Middle Ages inherited it from antiquity and bequeathed it to the Renaissance. The statement that the medieval Church frowned upon this discipline is often taken in a sense that makes it untrue. Orthodox theologians could accept the theory that the planets had an effect on events and on psychology, and, much more, on plants and minerals. It was not against this that the Church fought. She fought against three of its offshoots.

(1) Against the lucrative, and politically undesirable, practice of astrologically grounded predictions.

(2) Against astrological determinism. The doctrine of influences could be carried so far as to exclude free will. Against this determinism, as in later ages against other forms of determinism, theology had to make a defence. Aquinas treats the question very clearly.[2] On the physical side the influence of the spheres is unquestioned. Celestial bodies affect terrestrial bodies, including those of men. And by affecting our bodies they can, but need not, affect our reason and our will. They can, because our

---

[1] By A. Pannecock, *History of Astronomy* (1961).
[2] *Summa*, 1ᵃ, cxv, Art. 4.

higher faculties certainly receive something (*accipiunt*) from our lower. They need not, because any alteration of our imaginative power[1] produced in this way generates, not a necessity, but only a propensity, to act thus or thus. The propensity can be resisted; hence the wise man will over-rule the stars. But more often it will not be resisted, for most men are not wise; hence, like actuarial predictions, astrological predictions about the behaviour of large masses of men will often be verified.

(3) Against practices that might seem to imply or encourage the worship of planets—they had, after all, been the hardiest of all the Pagan gods. Albertus Magnus gives rulings about the lawful and unlawful use of planetary images in agriculture. The burial in your field of a plate inscribed with the character or hieroglyph of a planet is permissible; to use with it invocations or 'suffumigations' is not (*Speculum Astronomiae*, x).

Despite this careful watch against planetolatry the planets continued to be called by their divine names, and their representations in art and poetry are all derived from the Pagan poets—not, till later, from Pagan sculptors. The results are sometimes comic. The ancients had described Mars fully armed and in his chariot; medieval artists, translating this image into contemporary terms, accordingly depict him as a knight in plate armour seated in a farm-wagon[2]—which may have suggested the story in Chrétien's *Lancelot*. Modern readers sometimes

---

[1] Cf. Dante, *Purg.* XVII, 13-17.

[2] See J. Seznec, *The Survival of the Pagan Gods*, trans. B. F. Sessions (New York, 1953), p. 191.

discuss whether, when Jupiter or Venus is mentioned by a medieval poet, he means the planet or the deity. It is doubtful whether the question usually admits of an answer. Certainly we must never assume without special evidence that such personages are in Gower or Chaucer the merely mythological figures they are in Shelley or Keats. They are planets as well as gods. Not that the Christian poet believed in the god because he believed in the planet; but all three things—the visible planet in the sky, the source of influence, and the god—generally acted as a unity upon his mind. I have not found evidence that theologians were at all disquieted by this state of affairs.

Readers who already know the characters of the seven planets can skip the following list:

Saturn. In the earth his influence produces lead; in men, the melancholy complexion; in history, disastrous events. In Dante his sphere is the Heaven of contemplatives. He is connected with sickness and old age. Our traditional picture of Father Time with the scythe is derived from earlier pictures of Saturn. A good account of his activities in promoting fatal accidents, pestilence, treacheries, and ill luck in general, occurs in *The Knight's Tale* (A 2463 *sq.*). He is the most terrible of the seven and is sometimes called The Greater Infortune, *Infortuna Major*.

Jupiter, the King, produces in the earth, rather disappointingly, tin; this shining metal said different things to the imagination before the canning industry came in. The character he produces in men would now be very imperfectly expressed by the word 'jovial', and is not very easy to grasp; it is no longer, like the saturnine character, one of our archetypes. We may say it is *Kingly*; but we must think of a King at peace, enthroned, taking his leisure, serene. The Jovial character is cheerful, festive yet temperate, tranquil, magnanimous. When this planet dominates we may expect halcyon days and prosperity. In Dante wise and just princes go to his sphere when they die. He is the best planet, and is called The Greater Fortune, *Fortuna Major*.

Mars makes iron. He gives men the martial temperament, 'sturdy hardiness', as the Wife of Bath calls it (D612). But he is a bad planet, *Infortuna Minor*. He causes wars. His sphere, in Dante, is the Heaven of martyrs; partly for the obvious reason but partly, I suspect, because of a mistaken philological connection between *martyr* and *Martem*.

Sol is the point at which the concordat between the mythical and the astrological nearly breaks down. Mythically, Jupiter is the King, but Sol produces the noblest metal, gold, and is the eye and mind of the whole universe. He makes men wise and liberal and his sphere is the Heaven of theologians and philosophers. Though he is no more metallurgical than any other planet his metallurgical operations are more often mentioned than theirs. We read in Donne's *Allophanes and Idios* how soils which the Sun could make into gold may lie too far from the surface for his beams to take effect (61). Spenser's Mammon brings his hoard out to 'sun' it. If it were already gold, he would have no motive for doing this. It is still hore (grey); he suns it that it may become gold.[1] Sol produces fortunate events.

[1] *F.Q.*, versicle to II, vii.

In beneficence Venus stands second only to Jupiter; she is *Fortuna Minor*. Her metal is copper. The connection is not clear till we observe that Cyprus was once famed for its copper mines; that copper is *cyprium*, the Cyprian metal; and that Venus, or Aphrodite, especially worshipped in that island, was Κύπρις, the Lady of Cyprus. In mortals she produces beauty and amorousness; in history, fortunate events. Dante makes her sphere the Heaven not, as we might expect from a more obvious poet, of the charitable, but of those, now penitent, who in this life loved greatly and lawlessly. Here he meets Cunizza, four times a wife and twice a mistress, and Rahab the harlot (*Paradiso*, IX). They are in swift, incessant flight (VIII, 19–27)—a likeness in unlikeness to the impenitent and storm-borne lovers of *Inferno*, V.

Mercury produces quicksilver. Dante gives his sphere to beneficent men of action. Isidore, on the other hand, says this planet is called Mercurius because he is the patron of profit (*mercibus praeest*).[1] Gower says that the man born under Mercury will be 'studious' and 'in writinge curious',

> bot yit with somdel besinesse
> his hert is set upon richesse.

> (*Confessio*, VII, 765.)

The Wife of Bath associates him especially with clerks (D 706). In Martianus Capella's *De Nuptiis*[2] he is the bridegroom of Philologia—who is Learning or even Literature rather than what we call 'philology'. And I am

---

[1] See Augustine, *De Civitate*, VII, xiv.
[2] *De Nuptiis Philologiae et Mercurii*, ed. F. Eyssenhardt (Lipsiae, 1866).

pretty sure that 'the Words of Mercury' contrasted with 'the Songs of Apollo' at the end of *Love's Labour's Lost* are 'picked', or rhetorical prose. It is difficult to see the unity in all these characteristics. 'Skilled eagerness' or 'bright alacrity' is the best I can do. But it is better just to take some real mercury in a saucer and play with it for a few minutes. *That* is what 'Mercurial' means.

At Luna we cross in our descent the great frontier which I have so often had to mention; from aether to air, from 'heaven' to 'nature', from the realm of gods (or angels) to that of daemons, from the realm of necessity to that of contingence, from the incorruptible to the corruptible. Unless this 'great divide' is firmly fixed in our minds, every passage in Donne or Drayton or whom you will that mentions 'translunary' and 'sublunary' will lose its intended force. We shall take 'under the moon' as a vague synonym, like our 'under the sun', for 'everywhere', when in reality it is used with precision. When Gower says

> We that dwelle under the Mone
> Stand in this world upon a weer
>
> (*Confessio*, Prol. 142)

he means exactly what he says. If we lived above the Moon we should not suffer *weer* (doubt, uncertainty). When Chaucer's Nature says

> Ech thing in my cure is
> Under the Moone that mai wane and waxe
>
> (*Canterbury Tales*, C 22)

she is distinguishing her mutable realm from the translunary world where nothing grows or decreases. When

Chaucer says 'Fortune may non angel dere' in the *Monk's Tale* (B 3191) he is remembering that angels inhabit the aetherial realm where there is no contingence and therefore no luck, whether good or bad.

Her metal is silver. In men she produces wandering, and that in two senses. She may make them travellers so that, as Gower says, the man born under Luna will 'seche manye londes strange' (VII, 747). In this respect the English and the Germans are much under her influence (*ibid.* 751–4). But she may also produce 'wandering' of the wits, especially that periodical insanity which was first meant by the word *lunacy*, in which the patient, as Langland says (C X, 107), is 'mad as the mone sit, more other lasse'. These are the 'dangerous, unsafe lunes' of the *Winter's Tale* (II, ii, 30); whence (and on other grounds) *lunes* in *Hamlet* (III, iii, 7) is an almost certain emendation for Quarto's meaningless *browes* and Folio's unmetrical *lunacies*. Dante assigns the Moon's sphere to those who have entered the conventual life and abandoned it for some good or pardonable reason.

It will be noticed that while we find no difficulty in grasping the character of Saturn or Venus, Jove and Mercury almost evaded us. The truth which emerges from this is that the planetary characters need to be seized in an intuition rather than built up out of concepts; we need to know them, not to know about them, *connaître* not *savoir*. Sometimes the old intuitions survive; when they do not, we falter. Changes of outlook, which have left almost intact, and almost one, the character of Venus, have almost annihilated Jupiter.

In accordance with the principle of devolution or mediation the influences do not work upon us directly, but by first modifying the air. As Donne says in *The Extasie*, 'On man heaven's influence works not so But that it first imprints the air'. A pestilence is caused originally by malefical conjunctions of planets, as when

> Kinde herde tho Conscience and cam out of the planetes
> And sente forth his forayers, fevers and fluxes.
> (*Piers Plowman*, c. XXIII, 80.)

But the bad influence operates by being literally 'in the air'. Hence when a medieval doctor could give no more particular cause for the patient's condition he attributed it to 'this influence which is at present in the air'. If he were an Italian doctor he would doubtless say *questa influenza*. The profession has retained the useful word ever since.

It is always necessary to remember that *constellation* in medieval language seldom means, as with us, a permanent pattern of stars. It usually means a temporary state of their relative positions. The artist who had made the brazen horse in the *Squire's Tale* 'wayted many a constellacioun' (F 129). We should translate 'looked out for many a conjunction'.

The word *influence* in its modern sense—the sense in which this study has so often forced me to use it—is as grey an abstraction as the whole range of our language affords. We must take great care not to read this, the word's withered senility, back into its use by older poets where it is still a fully conscious metaphor from astrology. The ladies in *L'Allegro* (121) 'whose bright eyes Rain influence' are being compared with the planets. When Adam says to Eve

> I from the influence of thy lookes receave
> Access in every vertue.   (*Paradise Lost*, IX, 309)

he is saying far more than a modern reader might suppose. He is making himself an Earth, and her a Jove or Venus.

Two traits remain to be added to our picture.

Nothing is more deeply impressed on the cosmic imaginings of a modern than the idea that the heavenly bodies move in a pitch-black and dead-cold vacuity. It was not so in the Medieval Model. Already in our passage from Lucan[1] we have seen that (on the most probable interpretation) the ascending spirit passes into a region compared with which our terrestrial day is only a sort of night; and nowhere in medieval literature have I found any suggestion that, if we could enter the translunary world, we should find ourselves in an abyss of darkness. For their system is in one sense more heliocentric than ours. The sun illuminates the whole universe. All the stars, says Isidore (III, lxi) are said to have no light of their own but, like the Moon, to be illuminated by Sol. Dante in the *Convivio* agrees (II, xiii, 15). And as they had, I think, no conception of the part which the air plays in turning physical light into the circumambient colour-realm that we call Day, we must picture all the countless cubic miles within the vast concavity as illuminated. Night is merely the conical shadow cast by our Earth. It extends, according to Dante (*Paradiso*, IX, 118) as far as to the

---

[1] See above, p. 33. Cf. also Pliny, *Nat. Hist.* II, vii.

sphere of Venus. Since the Sun moves and the Earth is stationary, we must picture this long, black finger perpetually revolving like the hand of a clock; that is why Milton calls it 'the circling canopie of Night's extended shade' (*Paradise Lost*, III, 556). Beyond that there is no night; only 'happie climes that lie where day never shuts his eye' (*Comus*, 978). When we look up at the night sky we are looking through darkness but not at darkness.

And secondly, as that vast (though finite) space is not dark, so neither is it silent. If our ears were opened we should perceive, as Henryson puts it,

> every planet in his proper sphere
> In moving makand harmony and sound
>
> (*Fables*, 1659)

as Dante heard it (*Paradiso*, I, 78) and Troilus (V, 1812).

If the reader cares to repeat the experiment, already suggested, of a nocturnal walk with the medieval astronomy in mind, he will easily feel the effect of these two last details. The 'silence' which frightened Pascal was, according to the Model, wholly illusory; and the sky looks black only because we are seeing it through the dark glass of our own shadow. You must conceive yourself looking up at a world lighted, warmed, and resonant with music.

Much could still be added. But I omit the Signs, the Epicycles, and the Ecliptic. They contribute less to the emotional effect (which is my chief concern) and can hardly be made intelligible without diagrams.

The Heavens

C. THEIR INHABITANTS

God, we have said, causes the *Primum Mobile* to rotate. A modern Theist would hardly raise the question 'How?' But the question had been both raised and answered long before the Middle Ages, and the answer was incorporated in the Medieval Model. It was obvious to Aristotle that most things which move do so because some other moving object impels them. A hand, itself in motion, moves a sword; a wind, itself in motion, moves a ship. But it was also fundamental to his thought that no infinite series can be actual. We cannot therefore go on explaining one movement by another *ad infinitum*. There must in the last resort be something which, motionless itself, initiates the motion of all other things. Such a Prime Mover he finds in the wholly transcendent and immaterial God who 'occupies no place and is not affected by time'.[1] But we must not imagine Him moving things by any positive action, for that would be to attribute some kind of motion to Himself and we should then not have reached an utterly unmoving Mover. How then does He move things? Aristotle answers, κινεῖ ὡς ἐρώμενον, 'He moves as beloved'.[2] He moves other things, that is, as an object of desire moves those who desire it. The *Primum Mobile* is moved by its love for God, and, being moved, communicates motion to the rest of the universe.

It would be easy to descant on the antithesis between this Theology and that which is characteristic of Judaism (at its best) and Christianity. Both can speak about the

[1] See above, p. 96. [2] *Metaphysics*, 1072ᵇ.

'love of God'. But in the one this means the thirsty and aspiring love of creatures for Him; in the other, His provident and descending love for them. The antithesis should not, however, be regarded as a contradiction. A real universe could accommodate the 'love of God' in both senses. Aristotle describes the natural order, which is perpetually exhibited in the uncorrupted and translunary world. St John ('herein is love, not that we loved God, but that he loved us')[1] describes the order of Grace which comes into play here on earth because men have fallen. It will be noticed that when Dante ends the *Comedy* with 'the love that moves the Sun and the other stars', he is speaking of love in the Aristotelian sense.

But, while there is no contradiction, the antithesis fully explains why the Model is so little in evidence among spiritual writers and why the whole atmosphere of their work is so different from that of Jean de Meung or even Dante himself. Spiritual books are wholly practical in purpose, addressed to those who ask direction. Only the order of Grace is relevant.

Granted that the spheres are moved by love for God, a modern may still ask why this movement should take the form of rotation. To any ancient or medieval mind I believe the answer would have been obvious. Love seeks to participate in its object, to become as like its object as it can. But finite and created beings can never fully share the motionless ubiquity of God, just as time, however it multiplies its transitory presents, can never achieve the *totum simul* of eternity. The nearest approach to the

[1] I John iv. 10.

divine and perfect ubiquity that the spheres can attain is the swiftest and most regular possible movement, in the most perfect form, which is circular. Each sphere attains it in a less degree than the sphere above it, and therefore has a slower pace.

This all implies that each sphere, or something resident in each sphere, is a conscious and intellectual being, moved by 'intellectual love' of God. And so it is. These lofty creatures are called Intelligences. The relation between the Intelligence of a sphere and the sphere itself as a physical object was variously conceived. The older view was that the Intelligence is 'in' the sphere as the soul is 'in' the body, so that the planets are, as Plato would have agreed, ζῷα—celestial animals, animate bodies or incarnate minds. Hence Donne, speaking of our own bodies, can say 'We are The intelligences,[1] they the spheare'. Later, the Scholastics thought differently. 'We confess with the sacred writers', says Albertus Magnus,[2] 'that the heavens have not souls and are not animals if the word *soul* is taken in its strict sense. But if we wish to bring the scientists (*philosophos*) into agreement with the sacred writers, we can say that there are certain Intelligences in the spheres... and they are called the souls of the spheres... but they are not related to the spheres in that mode which justifies us in calling the (human) soul the entelechy of the body. We have spoken according to the scientists, who contradict the sacred writers only in name.' Aquinas[3]

---

[1] *The Extasie*, 51.
[2] *Summa de Creaturis* I[a], Tract. III, Quaest. XVI, Art. 2.
[3] I[a], LXX, Art. 3.

follows Albertus. 'Between those who hold that they are animals and those who do not, little or no difference is to be found in substance, but only in language (*in voce tantum*).'

The planetary Intelligences, however, make a very small part of the angelic population which inhabits, as its 'kindly stede', the vast aetherial region between the Moon and the *Primum Mobile*. Their graded species have already been described.

All this time we are describing the universe spread out in space; dignity, power and speed progressively diminishing as we descend from its circumference to its centre, the Earth. But I have already hinted that the intelligible universe reverses it all; there the Earth is the rim, the outside edge where being fades away on the border of nonentity. A few astonishing lines from the *Paradiso* (XXVIII, 25 *sq.*) stamp this on the mind forever. There Dante sees God as a point of light. Seven concentric rings of light revolve about that point, and that which is smallest and nearest to it has the swiftest movement. This is the Intelligence of the *Primum Mobile*, superior to all the rest in love and knowledge. The universe is thus, when our minds are sufficiently freed from the senses, turned inside out. Dante, with incomparably greater power is, however, saying no more than Alanus says when he locates us and our Earth 'outside the city wall'.

It may well be asked how, in that unfallen translunary world, there come to be such things as 'bad' or 'malefical' planets. But they are bad only in relation to us. On the psychological side this answer is implicit in Dante's allocation of blessed souls to their various planets after death. The temperament derived from each planet can be turned either to a good or a bad use. Born under Saturn, you are qualified to become either a mope and a malcontent or a great contemplative; under Mars, either an Attila or a martyr. Even the misuse of the psychology imposed on you by your stars can, through repentance, lead to its own appropriate species of beatitude; as in Dante's Cunizza. The other bad effects of the 'infortunes' —the plagues and disasters—can no doubt be dealt with in the same way. The fault lies not in the influence but in the terrestrial nature which receives it. In a fallen Earth it is permitted by Divine justice that we and our Earth and air respond thus disastrously to influences which are good in themselves. 'Bad' influences are those of which our corrupt world can no longer make a good use; the bad patient makes the agent bad in effect. The fullest account of this which I have met comes in a late and condemned book; but not, I presume, condemned on this score. It is the *Cantica Tria* of Franciscus Georgius Venetus (*ob.* 1540).[1] If all things here below were rightly disposed to the heavens, all influences, as Trismegistus taught, would be extremely good (*optimos*). When an evil effect follows them, this must be attributed to the ill-disposed subject (*indisposito subjecto*).[2]

But it is time we descended below the Moon, from the aether into the air. This, as the reader already knows, is the 'kindly stede' of the aerial beings, the daemons. In Laȝamon, who follows Apuleius, these creatures can be either good or bad. It is still so for Bernardus, who

[1] Parisiis, 1543. [2] *Cantici Primi*, tom. III, cap. 8.

divides the air into two regions, locating the good daemons in the upper and more tranquil part, the bad in the lower and more turbulent.[1] But as the Middle Ages went on the view gained ground that all daemons alike were bad; were in fact fallen angels or 'demons'. Alanus is taking this view when in *Anticlaudian* (IV, v) he speaks of the 'airish citizens' to whom the air is a prison; Chaucer remembered the passage.[2] Aquinas clearly equates daemons with devils.[3] The Pauline passage in Ephesians (ii. 2) about 'the prince of the powers of the air' probably had much to do with this, and also with the popular association between witchcraft and foul weather. Hence Milton's Satan in *Paradise Regained* calls the air 'our old conquest' (I, 46). But much doubt, as we shall see, still hung about the daemons, and Renaissance neo-Platonism revived the older conception, while Renaissance witch-hunters felt more and more confident about the new one. The Attendant Spirit in *Comus* is called the Daemon in the Trinity manuscript.

This much would suffice for daemons if we were at all sure that they confined themselves to the air and if they were never identified with creatures that bear a different name. I shall deal with those in the next chapter.

I can hardly hope that I shall persuade the reader to yet a third experimental walk by starlight. But perhaps, without actually taking the walk, he can now improve his picture of that old universe by adding such finishing touches as this section has suggested. Whatever else a

---

[1] *Op. cit.* II, *Pros.* VII, pp. 49–50.   [2] *Hous of Fame* II, 929.
[3] Iᵃ, LXIV, i, *et passim.*

modern feels when he looks at the night sky, he certainly feels that he is looking *out*—like one looking out from the saloon entrance on to the dark Atlantic or from the lighted porch upon dark and lonely moors. But if you accepted the Medieval Model you would feel like one looking *in*. The Earth is 'outside the city wall'. When the sun is up he dazzles us and we cannot see inside. Darkness, our own darkness, draws the veil and we catch a glimpse of the high pomps within; the vast, lighted concavity filled with music and life. And, looking in, we do not see, like Meredith's Lucifer, 'the army of unalterable law', but rather the revelry of insatiable love. We are watching the activity of creatures whose experience we can only lamely compare to that of one in the act of drinking, his thirst delighted yet not quenched. For in them the highest of faculties is always exercised without impediment on the noblest object; without satiety, since they can never completely make His perfection their own, yet never frustrated, since at every moment they approximate to Him in the fullest measure of which their nature is capable. You need not wonder that one old picture[1] represents the Intelligence of the *Primum Mobile* as a girl dancing and playing with her sphere as with a ball. Then, laying aside whatever Theology or Atheology you held before, run your mind up heaven by heaven to Him who is really the centre, to your senses the circumference, of all; the quarry whom all these untiring huntsmen pursue, the candle to whom all these moths move yet are not burned.

The picture is nothing if not religious. But is the

[1] Seznec, *op. cit.* p. 139.

religion in question precisely Christianity? Certainly there is a striking difference between this Model where God is much less the lover than the beloved and man is a marginal creature, and the Christian picture where the fall of man and the incarnation of God as man for man's redemption is central. There may perhaps, as I have hinted before, be no absolute logical contradiction. One may say that the Good Shepherd goes to seek the lost sheep because it is lost, not because it was the finest sheep in the flock. It may have been the least. But there remains, at the very least, a profound disharmony of atmospheres. That is why all this cosmology plays so small a part in the spiritual writers, and is not fused with high religious ardour in any writer I know except Dante himself. Another indication of the cleavage is this. We might expect that a universe so filled with shining super-human creatures would be a danger to monotheism. Yet the danger to monotheism in the Middle Ages clearly came not from a cult of angels but from the cult of the Saints. Men when they prayed were not usually thinking of the Hierarchies and Intelligences. There was, not (I think) an opposition, but a dissociation between their religious life and all that. At one point we might have expected contradiction. Is all this admirable universe, sinless and perfect everywhere beyond the Moon, to perish at the last day? It seems not. When scripture says the stars will fall (Matt. xxiv. 29) this may be taken 'tropically'; it may mean that tyrants and magnates will be brought low. Or the stars that will fall may be only meteorites. And St Peter (II Pet. iii. 3 *sq.*) says only that the universe will be destroyed by fire as it once was destroyed by water. But no one thinks the flood rose to the translunary regions: neither, then, need the fire.[1] Dante exempts the higher heavens from the final catastrophe; in *Paradiso*, VII, we learn that whatever flows immediately from God, *senza mezzo distilla* (67), will never end. The sublunary world was not created immediately; its elements were made by secondary agents. Man was made directly by God, hence his immortality; so were the angels, and apparently not only they but the *paese sincero nel qual tu sei* (130) 'this stainless realm where now thou art'. If this is taken literally, the translunary world will not be destroyed; it is only the (four) elements below the Moon which will perish 'with fervent heat'.

The human imagination has seldom had before it an object so sublimely ordered as the medieval cosmos. If it has an aesthetic fault, it is perhaps, for us who have known romanticism, a shade too ordered. For all its vast spaces it might in the end afflict us with a kind of claustrophobia. Is there nowhere any vagueness? No undiscovered byways? No twilight? Can we never get really out of doors? The next chapter will perhaps give us some relief.

[1] St Augustine, *De Civitate*, XX, xviii, xxiv. Aquinas, IIIª, Supplement, Q. LXXIV art. 4.

CHAPTER VI

THE *LONGAEVI*

There is something sinister about putting a leprechaun in the
workhouse. The only solid comfort is that he certainly will not
work.   CHESTERTON

I have put the *Longaevi* or longlivers into a separate chapter because their place of residence is ambiguous between
air and Earth. Whether they are important enough to
justify this arrangement is another question. In a sense, if
I may risk the oxymoron, their unimportance is their
importance. They are marginal, fugitive creatures. They
are perhaps the only creatures to whom the Model does
not assign, as it were, an official status. Herein lies their
imaginative value. They soften the classic severity of the
huge design. They intrude a welcome hint of wildness
and uncertainty into a universe that is in danger of being
a little too self-explanatory, too luminous.

I take for them the name *Longaevi* from Martianus
Capella, who mentions 'dancing companies of *Longaevi*
who haunt woods, glades, and groves, and lakes and
springs and brooks; whose names are Pans, Fauns...
Satyrs, Silvans, Nymphs...'.[1] Bernardus Silvestris, without using the word *Longaevi*, describes similar creatures—
'Silvans, Pans, and Nerei'—as having 'a longer life'
(than ours), though they are not immortal. They are
innocent—'of blameless conversation'—and have bodies
of elemental purity.[2]

---

[1] *De Nuptiis Mercurii et Philologiae*, ed. F. Eyssenhardt (Lipsiae, 1866),
II, 167, p. 45.   [2] *Op. cit.* II *Pros.* VII, p. 50.

The Longaevi

The alternative would have been to call them Fairies. But that word, tarnished by pantomime and bad children's books with worse illustrations, would have been dangerous as the title of a chapter. It might encourage us to bring to the subject some ready-made, modern concept of a Fairy and to read the old texts in the light of it. Naturally, the proper method is the reverse; we must go to the texts with an open mind and learn from them what the word *fairy* meant to our ancestors.

A good point to begin at is provided by three passages from Milton:

(1)   No evil thing that walks by night
In fog or fire, by lake or moorish fen,
Blue meagre Hag or stubborn unlaid ghost—
No goblin or swart Faery of the mine.

(Comus, 432 sq.)

(2)   Like that Pigmean Race
Beyond the *Indian* Mount, or Faery Elves,
Whose midnight Revels, by a Forest side
Or Fountain some belated Peasant sees...

(Paradise Lost, I, 780 sq.)

(3)   And Ladies of th'*Hesperides*, that seem'd
Fairer than feign'd of old, or fabl'd since
Of Fairy Damsels met in Forest wide
By Knights of *Logres*, or of *Lyones*—

(Paradise Regained, II, 357 sq.)

Milton lived too late to be direct evidence for medieval beliefs. The value of the passages for us is that they show the complexity of the tradition which the Middle Ages had bequeathed to him and his public. The three extracts were probably never connected in Milton's mind. Each serves a different poetic purpose. In each he confidently expects from his readers a different response to the word *fairy*. They were equally conditioned to all three responses and could be relied on to make the right one at each place. Another, earlier and perhaps more striking, witness to this complexity is that within the same island and the same century Spenser could compliment Elizabeth I by identifying her with the Faerie Queene and a woman could be burned at Edinburgh in 1576 for 'repairing with' the fairies and the 'Queen of Elfame'.[1]

The 'swart Faery' in *Comus* is classified among horrors. This is one strand in the tradition. *Beowulf* ranks the elves (*ylfe*, 111) along with ettins and giants as the enemies of God. In the ballad of *Isabel and the Elf-Knight*, the elf-knight is a sort of Bluebeard. In Gower, the slanderer of Constance says that she is 'of faierie' because she has given birth to a monster (*Confessio*, II, 964 *sq.*). The *Catholicon Anglicum* of 1483 gives *lamia* and *eumenis* (fury) as the Latin for *elf*; Horman's *Vulgaria* (1519), *strix* and *lamia* for fairy. We are inclined to ask 'Why not *nympha*?' But *nymph* would not have mended matters. It also could be a name of terror to our ancestors. 'What are these so fayre fiendes that cause my hayres to stand upright?' cries Corsites in Lyly's *Endymion* (IV, iii), 'Hags! Out alas! Nymphs!!'. Drayton in *Mortimer to Queen Isabel* speaks of 'the dishevelled gastly sea-Nymph' (77). Athanasius Kircher says to an apparition 'Aie! I

---

[1] M. W. Latham, *The Elizabethan Fairies* (Columbia, 1940), p. 16. I am much indebted to this throughout.

fear ye be one of those daemons whom the ancients called Nymphs', and receives the reassurance, 'I am no Lilith nor lamia'.[1] Reginald Scot mentions fairies (and nymphs) among bugbears used to frighten children: 'Our mothers' maids have so terrified us with bull-beggars,[2] spirits, witches, urchins, elves, hags, fairies, satyrs, pans, faunes, sylens, tritons, centaurs, dwarfs, giants, nymphes, Incubus, Robin good fellow, the spoorn, the man in the oke, the fire-drake, the puckle, Tom Thombe, Tom tumbler boneles, and such other bugs.'[3]

This dark view of the Fairies gained ground, I think, in the sixteenth and the earlier seventeenth century—an unusually hag-ridden period. Holinshed did not find in Boece but added to him the suggestion that Macbeth's three temptresses might be 'some nymphs or fairies'. Nor has this dread ever since quite disappeared except where belief in the Fairies has also done so. I have myself stayed at a lonely place in Ireland which was said to be haunted both by a ghost and by the (euphemistically so called) 'good people'. But I was given to understand it was the fairies rather than the ghost that induced my neighbours to give it such a wide berth at night.

Reginald Scot's list of bugbears raises a point which is worth a short digression. Some studies of folklore are almost entirely concerned with the genealogy of beliefs, with the degeneration of gods into Fairies. It is a very legitimate and most interesting inquiry. But Scot's list

---

[1] *Iter Extaticum II qui et Mundi Subterranei Prodromos dicitur* (Romae, Typis Mascardi, MDCLVII), II, i.

[2] Bogies.　　　　[3] *Discouerie of Witchcraft* (1584), VII, xv.

shows that when we are asking what furniture our ancestors' minds contained and how they felt about it— always with a view to the better understanding of what they wrote—the question of origins is not very relevant. They might or might not know the sources of the shapes that haunted their imagination. Sometimes they certainly did. Giraldus Cambrensis knew that Morgan had once been a Celtic goddess, *dea quaedam phantastica* as he says in the *Speculum Ecclesiae* (II, ix); and so, perhaps from him, did the poet of *Gawain* (2452). And any well-read contemporary of Scot's would have known that his satyrs, Pans, and fauns were classical while his 'Tom thombe' and 'puckle' were not. But obviously it makes no difference; they all affected the mind in the same way. And if all really came through 'our mothers' maids' it is natural they should. The real question, then, would be why they affect us so differently. For I take it that most of us even today can understand how a man could dread witches or 'spirits' while most of us imagine that a meeting with a nymph or a Triton, if it were possible, would be delightful. The native figures are not, even now, quite so innocuous as the classical. I think the reason is that the classical figures stand further—certainly in time and perhaps in other ways too—even from our half-beliefs, and therefore from even our imagined fears. If Wordsworth found the idea of seeing Proteus rise from the sea attractive, this was partly because he felt perfectly certain he never would. He would have felt less certain of never seeing a ghost; in proportion less willing to see one.

The second Miltonic passage introduces us to a different conception of the Fairies. It is more familiar to us because Shakespeare, Drayton, and William Browne made a literary use of it; from their use descend the minute and almost insectal fairies of the debased modern convention with their antennae and gauzy wings. Milton's 'Faery Elves' are compared to the 'Pigmean Race'. So in the ballad of *The Wee Wee Man*,

> When we came to the stair foot
> Ladies were dancing jimp and sma.

Richard Bovet in his *Pandaemonium* (1684) speaks of the fairies 'appearing like men and women of a stature generally near the smaller size of man'. Burton mentions 'places in Germany where they do usually walk in little coats, some two feet long'.[1] A housemaid we had when I was a boy, who had seen them near Dundrum in County Down, described them as 'the size of children' (age unspecified).

But when we have said 'smaller than men' we can define the size of these Fairies no further. Solemn discussions as to whether they are merely dwarfish, or Lilliputian, or even insectal, are quite out of place; and that for a reason which crossed our path before.[2] As I then said, the visual imagination of medieval and earlier writers never for long worked to scale. Indeed I cannot think of any book before *Gulliver* that makes any serious attempt to do so. What are the relative sizes of Thor and the Giants in the Prose Edda? There is no answer. In cap. XLV a giant's

[1] Pt. I, 2, M. I, subs. 2.   [2] See above, pp. 101–2.

glove seems to the three gods a great hall, and the thumb of it a side-chamber which two of them use as a bedroom. This would make a god to a giant as a small fly to a man. But in the very next chapter Thor is dining with the giants and can lift up—though for a special reason he cannot drain—the drinking horn they hand him. When it was possible to write like that we can expect no coherent account of the elves' stature. And it remained possible for centuries. Even in passages whose main point, such as it is, consists of scaling things down, the wildest confusion prevails. Drayton in *Nimphidia* makes Oberon big enough to catch a wasp in his arms at line 201 and small enough to ride on an ant at line 242; he might as well have made him able both to lift an elephant and to ride a fox-terrier. I do not suggest that such an artificial work could in any case be expected to give reliable evidence about popular belief. The point is rather that no work written in a period when such inconsistencies were acceptable will provide such evidence; and that popular belief was probably itself as incurably vague and incoherent as the literature.

In this kind of Fairy the (unspecified) small size is less important than some other features. Milton's 'Faery Elves' are 'on thir mirth and dance Intent' (I, 786). The peasant has blundered upon them by chance. They have nothing to do with him nor he with them. The previous kind, the 'swart Faery of the Mine', might meet you intentionally, and, if so, his intentions would certainly be sinister; this kind not. They appear—often with no suggestion that they are smaller than men—in places where they might have expected no mortal to see them:

> And ofte in forme of womman in moni deorne[1] weie
> Me sicth[2] of hom gret companie bothe hoppe and pleie.[3]

In the Wife of Bath's Tale we have the dance again, and it vanishes at the approach of a human spectator (D 991 *sq.*). Spenser takes over the motif and makes his dancing graces vanish when Calidore intrudes upon their revels (*F.Q.* VI, x). Thomson in *The Castle of Indolence* (I, xxx) knows about the vanishing.

It is needless to stress the difference between such Fairies and those mentioned in *Comus* or Reginald Scot's *Discouerie*. It is true that even the second sort may be slightly alarming; the heart of Milton's peasant beats 'at once with joy and fear'. The vision startles by its otherness. But there is no horror or aversion on the human side. These creatures flee from man, not man from them; and the mortal who observes them (only so long as he remains unobserved himself) feels that he has committed a sort of trespass. His delight is that of seeing fortuitously—in a momentary glimpse—a gaiety and daintiness to which our own laborious life is simply irrelevant.

This kind was taken over, very dully by Drayton, brilliantly by Shakespeare, and worked up into a comic device which, from the first, has lost nearly all the flavour of popular belief. From Shakespeare, modified (I think) by Pope's sylphs, they descend with increasing prettifica-

---

[1] Secret.   [2] One sees.
[3] *South English Legendary*, ed. *cit.* vol. II, p. 410.

tion and triviality, till we reach the fairies whom children are supposed to enjoy; so far as my experience goes, erroneously.

With the 'Fairy Damsels' of our third Miltonic passage we reach a kind of Fairy who is more important for the reader of medieval literature and less familiar to modern imagination. And it demands from us the most difficult response.

The Fairy Damsels are 'met in forest wide'. *Met* is the important word. The encounter is not accidental. They have come to find us, and their intentions are usually (not always) amorous. They are the *fées* of French romance, the *fays* of our own, the *fate* of the Italians. Launfal's mistress, the lady who carried off Thomas the Rymer, the fairies in *Orfeo*, Bercilak in *Gawain* (who is called 'an alvish man' at line 681), are of this kind. Morgan le Fay in Malory has been humanised; her Italian equivalent *Fata Morgana* is a full Fairy. Merlin—only half human by blood and never shown practising magic *as an art*—almost belongs to this order. They are usually of at least fully human stature. The exception is Oberon in *Huon of Bordeaux* who is dwarfish, but in virtue of his beauty, gravity, and almost numinous character, must be classified among (let us call them) the High Fairies.

These High Fairies display a combination of characteristics which we do not easily digest.

On the one hand, whenever they are described we are struck by their hard, bright, and vividly material splendour. We may begin, not with a real Fairy, but with one who merely looked as though he came 'of faerie', from

the fairy realm. This is the young lady-killer in Gower
(v, 7073). He is curled and combed and crowned with a
garland of green leaves; in a word, 'very well turned out'.
But the High Fairies themselves are very much more so.
Where a modern might expect the mysterious and the
shadowy he meets a blaze of wealth and luxury. The
Fairy King in *Sir Orfeo* comes with over a hundred knights
and a hundred ladies, on white horses. His crown consists of a single huge gem as bright as the sun (142–52).
When we follow him to his own country we find there
nothing shadowy or unsubstantial; we find a castle that
shines like crystal, a hundred towers, a good moat,
buttresses of gold, rich carvings (355 *sq.*). In *Thomas the
Rymer* the Fairy wears green silk and a velvet mantle, and
her horse's mane jingles with fifty-nine silver bells.
Bercilak's costly clothes and equipment are described
with almost fulsome detail in *Gawain* (151–220). The
Fairy in *Sir Launfal* has dressed her waiting women in
'Inde sandel', green velvet embroidered with gold, and
coronets each containing more than sixty precious stones
(232–9). Her pavilion is of Saracenic work, the knobs on
the tent-poles are of crystal, and the whole is surmounted
by a golden eagle so enriched with enamel and carbuncles
that neither Alexander nor Arthur had anything so
precious (266–76).

In all this one may suspect a certain vulgarity of
imagination—as if to be a High Fairy were much the same
as being a millionaire. Nor does it obviously mend matters
to remind ourselves that Heaven and the saints were often
pictured in very similar terms. Undoubtedly it is *naïf*; but

the charge of vulgarity perhaps involves a misapprehension. Luxury and material splendour in the modern world need be connected with nothing but money and are also, more often than not, very ugly. But what a medieval man saw in royal or feudal courts and imagined as being outstripped in 'faerie' and far outstripped in Heaven, was not so. The architecture, arms, crowns, clothes, horses, and music were nearly all beautiful. They were all symbolical or significant—of sanctity, authority, valour, noble lineage or, at the very worst, of power. They were associated, as modern luxury is not, with graciousness and courtesy. They could therefore be ingenuously admired without degradation for the admirer.

Such, then, is one characteristic of the High Fairies. But despite this material splendour, shown to us in full light and almost photographically detailed, they can at any moment be as elusive as those 'Faery Elves' who are glimpsed dancing 'by a forest side or fountain'. Orfeo awaits the Fairy King with a guard of a thousand knights, but it is all no use. His wife is carried off, no one sees how—'with fairi forth ynome' and 'men wist never wher she was bicome' (193-4). Before we see the Fairies again, in their own realm, they have faded to a 'dim cri and blowing' heard far off in the woods. Launfal's mistress can be met only in secret, in 'derne stede'; there she will come to him, but no one will see her coming (353 *sq.*).

But she is very palpable flesh and blood when she is there. The High Fairies are vital, energetic, wilful, passionate beings. Launfal's Fairy lies in her rich pavilion naked down to the waist, white as a lily, red as a rose. Her first words demand his love. An excellent lunch follows, and then to bed (289–348). Thomas the Rymer's Fairy shows herself, so far as ballad brevity allows, a stirring and sportive creature, 'a lady gay come out to hunt in her follee'. Bercilak is the best of all in his mingled ferocity and geniality, his complete mastery of every situation, his madcap mirth. Two descriptions of fairies, one from a later and one from an earlier period, come far nearer to the High Fairies of the Middle Ages than anything our modern imaginations would be likely to produce. A *rowdy* High Fairy would seem to us a kind of oxymoron. But Robert Kirk in his *Secret Commonwealth* (1691) calls some of these 'wights like furious hardie men'. And an old Irish poet describes them as routing battalions of enemies, devastating every land they attack, great killers, noisy in the beer-house, makers of songs.[1] One can imagine the Fairy King in *Sir Orfeo*, or Bercilak, feeling at home with these.

If we are to call the High Fairies in any sense 'spirits', we must take along with us Blake's warning that 'a Spirit and a Vision are not, as the modern philosophy supposes, a cloudy vapour or a nothing; they are organised and minutely articulated beyond all that the mortal and perishing nature can produce'.[2] And if we call them 'supernatural' we must be clear what we mean. Their life is, in one sense, *more* 'natural'—stronger, more reckless, less inhibited, more triumphantly and impenitently passionate—than ours. They are liberated both from the

[1] See L. Abercrombie, *Romanticism* (1926), p. 53.

[2] *Descriptive Catalogue*, IV.

beast's perpetual slavery to nutrition, self-protection and procreation, and also from the responsibilities, shames, scruples, and melancholy of Man. Perhaps also from death; but of that later.

Such, very briefly, are the three kinds of Fairies or *Longaevi* we meet in our older literature. How far, by how many, and how consistently, they were believed in, I do not know. But there was sufficient belief to produce rival theories of their nature; attempts, which never reached finality, to fit even these lawless vagrants into the Model. I will mention four.

(1) That they are a third rational species distinct from angels and men. This third species can be variously conceived. The 'Silvans, Pans and Nerei' of Bernardus, who live longer than we but not forever, are clearly a rational (and terrestrial) species distinct from our own, and such figures, for all their classical names, could be equated with Fairies. Hence Douglas in his *Eneados* glosses Virgil's *Fauni nymphaeque* (VIII, 314) with the line 'Quhilk fair folkis or than elvis cleping we'. The *fata* in Boiardo who explains that she, like all her kind, cannot die till Dooms-day comes,[1] implies the same conception. An alternative view could find the required third species among those spirits which, according to the principle of plenitude, existed in every element[2]—the 'spirits of every element' in *Faustus* (151), the 'Tetrarchs of Fire, Air, Flood, and on the Earth' in *Paradise Regained* (IV, 201). Shakespeare's Ariel, a figure incomparably more serious than any in the

[1] *Orlando Innamorato*, II, xxvi, 15.
[2] Ficino, *Theologia Platonica de Immortalitate*, IV, i.

The Longaevi

Dream, would be a tetrarch of air. The most precise account of the elementals would, however, leave only one of their kinds to be strictly identified with the Fairies. Paracelsus[1] enumerates: (*a*) *Nymphae* or *Undinae*, of water, who are human in stature, and talk. (*b*) *Sylphi* or *Silvestres*, of air. They are larger than men and don't speak. (*c*) *Gnomi* or *Pygmaei*, of earth: about two spans high and extremely taciturn. (*d*) *Salamandrae* or *Vulcani*, of fire. The Nymphs or Undines are clearly Fairies. The Gnomes are closer to the Dwarfs of *märchen*. Paracelsus would be rather too late an author for my purpose if there were not reason to suppose that he is, in part anyway, using much earlier folklore. In the fourteenth century the family of Lusignan boasted a water-spirit among their ancestresses.[2] Later still we get the theory of a third rational species with no attempt to identify it. The *Discourse concerning Devils and Spirits*, added in 1665 to Scot's *Discouerie*, says 'their nature is middle between Heaven and Hell...they reign in a third kingdom, having no other judgement or doom to expect forever'. Finally, Kirk in his *Secret Commonwealth* identifies them with those aerial people whom I have had to mention so often already: 'of a middle nature between Man and Angel, as were Daemons thought to be of old'.

(2) That they are angels, but a special class of angels who have been, in our jargon, 'demoted'. This view is developed at some length in the *South English Legendary*.[3]

---

[1] *De Nymphis*, etc., 1, 2, 3, 6.
[2] S. Runciman, *History of the Crusades* (1954), vol. II, p. 424.
[3] Vol. II, pp. 408–10.

When Lucifer rebelled, he and his followers were cast into Hell. But there were also angels who 'somdel with him hulde': fellow-travellers who did not actually join the rebellion. These were banished into the lower and more turbulent levels of the airy region. They remain there till Doomsday, after which they go to Hell. And thirdly there was what I suppose we might call a party of the centre; angels who were only 'somdel in misthought'; almost, but not quite, guilty of sedition. These were banished, some to the higher and calmer levels of air, some to various places on earth, including the Earthly Paradise. Both the second and the third group sometimes communicate with men in dreams. Of those whom mortals have seen dancing and called *eluene* many will return to Heaven at Doomsday.

(3) That they are the dead, or some special class of the dead. At the end of the twelfth century, Walter Map in his *De Nugis Curialium* twice[1] tells the following story. There was in his time a family known as The Dead Woman's Sons (*filii mortuae*). A Breton knight had buried his wife, who was really and truly dead—*re vera mortuam*. Later, by night, passing through a lonely valley, he saw her alive amidst a great company of ladies. He was frightened, and wondered what was being done 'by the Fairies' (*a fatis*), but he snatched her from them and carried her off. She lived happily with him for several years and bore children. Similarly in Gower's story of Rosiphelee[2] the company of ladies, who are in all respects exactly like High Fairies, turn out to be dead women.

[1] II, xiii; IV, viii. [2] IV, 1245 *sq.*

Boccaccio tells the same story, and Dryden borrowed it from him in his *Theodore and Honoria*. In *Thomas the Rymer*, it will be remembered, the Fairy brings Thomas to a place where the road divides into three, leading respectively to Heaven, Hell, and 'fair Elfland'. Of those who reach the latter some will finally go to Hell, for the Devil has a right to 10 per cent of them every seventh year. In *Orfeo* the poet seems quite unable to make up his mind whether the place to which the Fairies have taken Dame Heurodis is or is not the land of the dead. At first all seems plain sailing. It is full of people who had been supposed dead and weren't (389–90). That is imaginable; some whom we think dead are only 'with the faerie'. But next moment it appears to be full of people who had really died; the beheaded, the strangled, the drowned, those who died in childbed (391–400). Then we revert to those who in their sleep were taken thither by Fairies (401–4).

The identity, or close connection between the Fairies and the dead was certainly believed in, for witches confessed to seeing the dead among the Fairies.[1] Answers to leading questions under torture naturally tell us nothing about the beliefs of the accused; but they are good evidence for the beliefs of the accusers.

(4) That they are fallen angels; in other words, devils. This becomes almost the official view after the accession of James I. 'That kinde of Devils conversing in the earth', he says (*Daemonologie*, III, i) 'may be divided in foure different kindes...the fourth is these kinde of spirites

---

[1] Latham, *op. cit.* p. 46.

that are called vulgarlie the Fayrie'. Burton includes among terrestrial devils 'Lares, Genii, Fauns, Satyrs, Wood-Nymphs, Foliots, Fairies, Robin Good-fellow, Trulli, etc.'[1]

This view, which is closely connected with the later Renaissance phobia about witches, goes far to explain the degradation of the Fairies from their medieval vitality into the kickshaws of Drayton or William Browne. A churchyard or a brimstone smell came to hang about any treatment of them which was not obviously playful. Shakespeare may have had practical as well as poetical reasons for making Oberon assure us that he and his fellows are 'spirits of another sort' than those who have to vanish at daybreak (*Dream*, III, ii, 388). One might have expected the High Fairies to have been expelled by science; I think they were actually expelled by a darkening of superstition.

Such were the efforts to find a socket into which the Fairies would fit. No agreement was achieved. As long as the Fairies remained at all they remained evasive.

[1] Pt. I, s. 2; M. I, subs. 2.

EARTH AND HER INHABITANTS

In tenui labor.
VIRGIL

A. THE EARTH

We have already seen that all below the Moon is mutable and contingent. We have also seen that each of the celestial spheres is guided by an Intelligence. Since Earth does not move and therefore needs no guidance, it was not generally felt that an Intelligence need be assigned to her. It was left, so far as I know, for Dante to make the brilliant suggestion that she has one after all and, that this terrestrial Intelligence is none other than Fortune. Fortune, to be sure, does not steer the Earth through an orbit; she fulfils the office of an Intelligence in the mode proper to a stationary globe. God, says Dante, who gave the heavens their guides 'so that every part communicates splendour to every other, equitably distributing light, likewise ordained a general minister and guide to worldly splendours; one who should from time to time transfer these deceptive benefits from one nation or stock to another in a fashion which no human wisdom can prevent. That is why one people rules while another grows weak.' For this she is much abused by mortal tongues, 'but she is blessed and never hears them. Happy among the other primal creatures, she turns her sphere and rejoices in her bliss.'[1] Ordinarily Fortune has a

[1] *Inferno*, VII, 73–96.

wheel; by making it a sphere Dante emphasises the new rank he has given her.

This is the ripe fruit of the Boethian doctrine. That contingency should reign in the fallen world below the Moon is not itself a contingent fact. Since worldly splendours are deceptive, it is fit that they should circulate. The pond must be continually stirred or it will become pestilential. The angel who stirs it rejoices in this action as the heavenly spheres rejoice in theirs.

The conception that the rise and fall of empires depends not on desert, nor on any 'trend' in the total evolution of humanity, but simply on the irresistible rough justice of Fortune, giving all their turns, did not pass away with the Middle Ages. 'All cannot be happy at once,' says Thomas Browne, 'for, because the glory of one state depends upon the ruins of another, there is a revolution and vicissitude of their greatness.'[1] We shall have to return to this point when we come to the medieval view of history.

Physically considered, the Earth is a globe; all the authors of the high Middle Ages are agreed on this. In the earlier 'Dark' Ages, as indeed in the nineteenth century, we can find Flat-earthers. Lecky,[2] whose purpose demanded some denigration of the past, has gleefully dug out of the sixth century Cosmas Indicopleustes who believed the Earth to be a flat parallelogram. But on Lecky's own showing Cosmas wrote partly to refute, in the supposed interests of religion, a prevalent, contrary view which believed in the Antipodes. Isidore gives Earth

[1] *Religio*, I, xvii.
[2] *Rise of Rationalism in Europe* (1887), vol. I, pp. 268 *sq.*

the shape of a wheel (XIV, ii, 1). And Snorre Sturlason thinks of it as the 'world-disc' or *heimskringla*—the first word, and hence the title, of his great saga. But Snorre writes from within the Norse enclave which was almost a separate culture, rich in native genius but half cut off from the Mediterranean legacy which the rest of Europe enjoyed.

The implications of a spherical Earth were fully grasped. What we call gravitation—for the medievals 'kindly enclyning'—was a matter of common knowledge. Vincent of Beauvais expounds it by asking what would happen if there were a hole bored through the globe of Earth so that there was a free passage from the one sky to the other, and someone dropped a stone down it. He answers that it would come to rest at the centre.[1] Temperature and momentum, I understand, would lead to a different result in fact, but Vincent is clearly right in principle. Mandeville in his *Voiage and Travaile* teaches the same truth more ingenuously: 'from what part of the earth that men dwell, either above or beneath, it seemeth always to them that dwell that they go more right than any other folk. And right as it seemeth to us that they be under us, right so it seemeth to them that we be under them' (xx). The most vivid presentation is by Dante, in a passage which shows that intense realising power which in the medieval imagination oddly co-exists with its feebleness in matters of scale. In *Inferno*, XXXIV, the two travellers find the shaggy and gigantic Lucifer at the absolute centre of the Earth, embedded up to his waist in

[1] *Speculum Naturale*, VII, vii.

ice. The only way they can continue their journey is by climbing down his sides—there is plenty of hair to hold on by—and squeezing through the hole in the ice and so coming to his feet. But they find that though it is *down* to his waist, it is *up* to his feet. As Virgil tells Dante, they have passed the point towards which all heavy objects move (70–111). It is the first 'science-fiction effect' in literature.

The erroneous notion that the medievals were Flat-earthers was common enough till recently. It might have two sources. One is that medieval maps, such as the great thirteenth-century *mappemounde* in Hereford cathedral, represent the Earth as a circle, which is what men would do if they believed it to be a disc. But what would men do if, knowing it was a globe and wishing to represent it in two dimensions, they had not yet mastered the late and difficult art of projection? Fortunately we need not answer this question. There is no reason to suppose that the *mappemounde* represents the whole surface of the Earth. The theory of the Four Zones[1] taught that the equatorial region was too hot for life. The other hemisphere of the Earth was to us wholly inaccessible. You could write science-fiction about it, but not geography. There could be no question of including it in a map. The *mappemounde* depicts the hemisphere we live in.

The second reason for the error might be that we find in medieval literature references to the world's end. Often these are as vague as similar references in our own

[1] See above, p. 28.

time. But they may be more precise, as when, in a geographical passage, Gower says

> Fro that into the worldes ende
> Estward, Asie it is. (VII, 568-9.)

But the same explanation might cover both this and the Hereford map. The 'world' of man, the only world that can ever concern us, may end where our hemisphere ends.

A glance at the Hereford *mappemounde* suggests that thirteenth-century Englishmen were almost totally ignorant of geography. But they cannot have been anything like so ignorant as the cartographer appears to be. For one thing the British Isles themselves are one of the most ludicrously erroneous parts of his map. Dozens, perhaps hundreds, of those who looked at it when it was new, must at least have known that Scotland and England were not separate islands; the blue bonnets had come over the border too often to permit any such illusion. And secondly, medieval man was by no means a static animal. Kings, armies, prelates, diplomats, merchants, and wandering scholars were continually on the move. Thanks to the popularity of pilgrimages even women, and women of the middle class, went far afield; witness the Wife of Bath and Margery Kempe. A practical knowledge of geography must have been pretty widely diffused. But it did not, I suspect, exist in the form of maps or even of map-like visual images. It would be an affair of winds to be waited for, landmarks to be picked up, capes to be doubled, this or that road to be taken at a fork. I doubt whether the maker of the *mappemounde* would have been at all disquieted to learn that many an illiterate sea-captain knew enough to refute his map in a dozen places. I doubt whether the sea-captain would have attempted to use his superior knowledge for any such purpose. A map of the whole hemisphere on so small a scale could never have been intended to have any practical use. The cartographer wished to make a rich jewel embodying the noble art of cosmography, with the Earthly Paradise marked as an island at the extreme Eastern edge (the East is at the top in this as in other medieval maps) and Jerusalem appropriately in the centre. Sailors themselves may have looked at it with admiration and delight. They were not going to steer by it.

A great deal of medieval geography is, none the less, merely romantic. Mandeville is an extreme example; but soberer authors are also concerned to fix the site of Paradise. The tradition which places it in the remote East seems to go back to a Jewish romance about Alexander, written before 500, and Latinised in the twelfth century as the *Iter ad Paradisum*.[1] This may underlie the *mappemounde*, and Gower (VII, 570), and also Mandeville who puts it beyond Prester John's country, beyond Taprobane (Ceylon), beyond the Dark Country (xxxiii). A later view puts it in Abyssinia; as Richard Eden says 'in the East side of Afrike beneath the red sea dwelleth the great and mighty Emperour and Christian King Prester John...in this province are many exceeding high mountains upon the which is said to be the earthly

[1] See G. Cary, *The Medieval Alexander* (1956).

paradise'.[1] Sometimes the rumour of a secret and delectable place on those mountains takes another form. Peter Heylin in his *Cosmography* (1652) says 'the hill of Amara is a day's journey high, on the top whereof are thirty-four palaces in which the younger sons of the Emperour are continually enclosed'. Milton, whose imagination absorbed like a sponge, combined both traditions in his 'Mount Amara' 'where Abassin kings their issue guard...by some suppos'd True Paradise' (*P.L.* IV, 280 *sq.*). Amara is used by Johnson for the Happy Valley in *Rasselas*. If it also suggested, as I suspect it did, Coleridge's 'Mount Abora', this remote mountain has deserved strangely well of English readers.

Side by side with these stories, however, the geographical knowledge of the medievals extended further East than we always remember. The Crusades, mercantile voyages, and pilgrimages—at some periods a highly organised industry—had opened the Levant. Franciscan missionaries had visited the Great Khan in 1246 and in 1254, when the meeting was at Karakorum. Nicolo and Maffeo Polo came to Kublai's court at Pekin in 1266; their more famous nephew Marco long resided there, returning in 1291. But the foundation of the Ming dynasty in 1368 largely put an end to such intercourse.

Marco Polo's great *Travels* (1295) is easily accessible and should be on everyone's shelves. At one point it has an interesting connection with our literature. Marco describes the Gobi desert as a place so haunted by evil spirits that travellers who lag behind 'until the caravan is

[1] *Briefe Description of Afrike* in Hakluyt.

no longer in sight' will be called to by their names and in some well-known voice. But if they follow the call they will be lost and perish (1, xxxvi). This also passes into Milton and becomes those

> airy tongues that syllable men's names
> On Sands and Shores and desert wildernesses.
>
> (*Comus*, 208–9.)

An interesting attempt has recently been made[1] to show that some real knowledge of the Atlantic islands and even of America lies behind the legend of St Brendan. But we need not discuss the case for this theory since, even if such knowledge existed, it has no general influence on the medieval mind. Explorers sailed west to find rich Cathay. If they had known that a huge, uncivilised continent lay between, they would probably not have sailed at all.

B. BEASTS

Compared with medieval Theology, philosophy, astronomy, or architecture, medieval zoology strikes us as childish; such zoology, at least, as they most often put into books. For, as there was a practical geography which had nothing to do with the *mappemounde*, so there was a practical zoology which had nothing to do with the Bestiaries. The percentage of the population who knew a great deal about certain animals must have been far larger in medieval than in modern England. It could not have been otherwise in a society where everyone who could be was a horseman, hunter, and hawker, and

[1] G. Ashe, *Land to the West* (1962).

everyone else a trapper, fisher, cowman, shepherd, swine-herd, goose-girl, henwife, or beekeeper. A good medieval-ist (A. J. Carlyle) once said in my hearing, 'The typical Knight of the Middle Ages was far more interested in pigs than in tournaments'. But all this first-hand knowledge appears very seldom in the texts. When it does—when, for example, the poet of *Gawain* assumes in his audience a familiarity with the anatomy of the deer (1325 *sq.*)—the laugh turns not against the Middle Ages but against our-selves. Such passages, however, are rare. The written zoology of their period is mainly a mass of cock-and-bull stories about creatures the authors had never seen, and often about creatures that never existed.

The merit of having invented, or the disgrace of having first believed, these fancies does not belong to the medievals. They are usually handing on what they received from the ancients. Aristotle, indeed, had laid the foundations of a genuinely scientific zoology; if he had been known first and followed exclusively we might have had no Bestiaries. But this was not what happened. From Herodotus down, the classics are full of travellers' tales about strange beasts and birds; tales too intriguing to be easily rejected. Aelian (second century B.C.) and the elder Pliny are storehouses of such matters. The medieval failure to distinguish between writers of wholly different kinds was also at work. Phaedrus (first century A.D.) was, in intention, merely writing Aesopic fables. But his dragon (IV, xx)—a creature born under evil stars, *dis iratis natus*, and doomed to guard against others the treasure it cannot use itself—would seem to be the ancestor of all those dragons whom we think so Germanic when we meet them in Anglo-Saxon and Old Norse. The image proved so potent an archetype that it engendered belief, and, even when belief faded, men were unwilling to let it go. In two thousand years western humanity has neither got tired of it nor improved it. Beowulf's dragon and Wagner's dragon are unmistakably the dragon of Phaedrus. (The Chinese dragon, I understand, is different.)

Many conductors, no doubt, not all of them now discoverable, helped to transmit such lore to the Middle Ages. Isidore is one of the most easily accessible. In him, moreover, we can see actually at work the process by which the pseudo-zoology grew up. His sections on the Horse are particularly instructive.

'Horses can scent battle; they are incited to war by the sound of the trumpet' (XII, i, 43). A highly lyrical passage from Job (xxxix. 19–25) is here being turned into a proposition in natural history. But we may not be quite out of touch with observation. Experienced cavalry chargers, especially stallions, probably do behave in some such way. We reach a further stage when Isidore tells us that the adder (*aspis*), to protect herself against snake-charmers, lies down and presses one ear to the ground and curls her tail round to stop up the other (XII, iv, 12) — patently a prosaic conversion into pseudo-science of the metaphor about the adder who 'stoppeth her ear' in Ps. lviii. 4–5.

'Horses shed tears on the death of their masters' (XII, i, 43). I take it the ultimate source is *Iliad*, XVII, 426 *sq.*, filtered to Isidore through *Aeneid*, XI, 90.

'Hence' (i.e. from this human trait in horses) 'in Centaurs the nature of horse and man is mixed' (*ibid.*). Here we have a timid attempt at rationalisation.

Then, in XII, i, 44–60, we plunge into matter of a very different sort. This long passage is all about the marks of a good horse, both in build and colour, and about breeds and breeding, and the like. This sounds to me as if some of it were really learned in the stable, as if grooms and dealers here replaced the literary *auctores*.

When *auctores* come into play, Isidore makes no kind of differentiation between them. The Bible, Cicero, Horace, Ovid, Martial, Pliny, Juvenal, and Lucan (the latter chiefly on snakes) all have for him exactly the same sort of authority. Yet his credulity has limits. He denies that weasels conceive by the mouth and bear by the ear (XII, iii, 3), and rejects the many-headed hydra as *fabulosus* (*ibid.* iv, 23).

One of the most remarkable things about Isidore is that he draws no morals from his beasts and gives them no allegorical interpretations. He says the Pelican revives its young by its own blood (XII, vii, 26) but draws no such parallel between this and the life-giving death of Christ as was later to produced the tremendous *Pie Pelicane*. He tells us, from unnamed 'writers on the nature of animals' (XII, ii, 13) that the unicorn is a beast too strong for any hunter to take; but if you set a virgin before him he loses all his ferocity, lays down his head in her lap, and sleeps. Then we can kill him. It is hard to believe that any Christian can think for long about this exquisite myth without seeing in it an allegory of the

Incarnation and Crucifixion. Yet Isidore makes no such suggestion.

The sort of interpretation which Isidore omits became the chief interest of pseudo-zoologists in the Middle Ages. The best remembered specimen is the author whom Chaucer calls Physiologus in the *Nun's Priest's Tale* (B 4459); really Theobald who was Abbot of Monte Cassino from 1022 to 1035 and wrote *Physiologus de Naturis XII Animalium*. But he was not the first, and certainly not the best, of his kind. The animal poems in the *Exeter Book* are older. The *Phoenix* in its earlier parts is paraphrased from Lactantius; the *moralitas* which the Anglo-Saxon poet added to this is thought to be based on St Ambrose and Bede; the *Panther* and *Whale*, on an older *Physiologus* in Latin.[1] As literature they are very much better than Theobald's work. Thus both the Anglo-Saxon and Theobald make the whale a type of the Devil. Sailors, says Theobald, mistake him for a promontory, land on him, and light a fire. Excusably, he dives and they are drowned. In the Anglo-Saxon they mistake him, more plausibly, for an island and he dives, not because he can feel the fire but through malice. The relief of the storm-tossed men on landing is vividly imagined: 'when the brute, skilled in ruses, perceives that the voyagers are fully settled and have pitched their tent, glad of fair weather, then of a sudden at all adventure down he goes into the salt flood' (19-27).

It is rather surprising to find the Siren, wrongly identified with the Mermaid, among Theobald's beasts. This way of classifying creatures that might otherwise claim to

[1] See G. P. Krapp, *Exeter Book* (1936), p. xxxv.

be *Longaevi* was not, I think, common in the Middle Ages. I have found it much later in Athanasius Kircher, who holds that such quasi- or semi-human forms are merely brutes (*rationis expertia*) whose resemblance to man is no more significant than that of the Mandrake. 'Or', he adds in happy ignorance of later biology,' that of the monkey.'[1]

It is even odder that Theobald should ignore the two creatures which we should have supposed the most fitted for his purpose: the Pelican and the Phoenix. But it is of a piece with the whole quality of his work. Either he had no imagination or an imagination whose wavelength evades us. I cannot face the weariness of going through his items one by one.[2] Whatever he has to say is said better in the vernacular Bestiaries.

These animal stories, like those of the Fairies, set us wondering how much was actually believed. Home-dwellers in an unscientific age will believe almost anything about foreign parts; but who could have believed, and how, what the Bestiaries told them about eagles, foxes, or stags? We can only guess at the answer. I am inclined to think that an absence of vocal and clearly held disbelief was commoner than a firm positive conviction. Most of those who helped either by speech or writing to keep the pseudo-zoology in circulation were not really concerned, one way or the other, with the question of fact; just as today the public speaker who warns me not to hide my

---

[1] *Mundi Subterranei Prodromos*, III, i.

[2] They are Lion, Eagle, Snake, Ant, Fox, Stag, Spider, Whale, Siren, Elephant, Turtle-dove, Panther.

head in the sand like an ostrich, is not really thinking, and does not want me to think, about ostriches. The *moralitas* is what matters. You need to 'know' these 'facts' in order to read the poets or take part in polite conversation. Hence, as Bacon said, 'if an untruth in nature be once on foot...by reason of the use of the opinion in similitudes and ornaments of speech, it is never called down'.[1] For to most men, as Browne puts it in *Vulgar Errors* 'a piece of Rhetorick is a sufficient argument of Logick; an Apologue of *Esop*, beyond a syllogysme in *Barbara*; parables than propositions, and proverbs more powerful than demonstrations' (I, iii). In the Middle Ages, and indeed later, we must add another source of credulity. If, as Platonism taught—nor would Browne himself have dissented—the visible world is made after an invisible pattern, if things below the Moon are all derived from things above her, the expectation that an anagogical or moral sense will have been built into the nature and behaviour of the creatures would not be *a priori* unreasonable. To us an account of animal behaviour would seem improbable if it suggested too obvious a moral. Not so to them. Their premises were different.

C. THE HUMAN SOUL

Man is a rational animal, and therefore a composite being, partly akin to the angels who are rational but—on the later, scholastic view—not animal, and partly akin to the beasts which are animal but not rational. This gives

[1] *Advancement*, I, Everyman, p. 70.

us one of the senses in which he is the 'little world' or
microcosm. Every mode of being in the whole universe
contributes to him; he is a cross-section of being. As
Gregory the Great (540–604) says, 'because man has
existence (*esse*) in common with stones, life with
trees, and understanding (*discernere*) with angels, he is
rightly called by the name of the world'.[1] This is almost
exactly reproduced by Alanus,[2] Jean de Meung,[3] and
Gower.[4]

Rational Soul, which gives man his peculiar position, is
not the only kind of soul. There are also Sensitive Soul and
Vegetable Soul. The powers of Vegetable Soul are
nutrition, growth and propagation. It alone is present in
plants. Sensitive Soul, which we find in animals, has
these powers but has sentience in addition. It thus
includes and goes beyond Vegetable Soul, so that a beast
can be said to have two levels of soul, Sensitive and
Vegetable, or a double soul, or even—though mislead-
ingly—two souls. Rational Soul similarly includes Vegetable and Sensitive, and adds reason. As Trevisa (1398),
translating the thirteenth-century *De Proprietatibus Rerum*
of Bartholomaeus Anglicus, puts it, there are 'thre manere
soulis...*vegetabilis* that geveth lif and no feling, *sensibilis*
that geveth lif and feling and nat resoun, *racionalis* that
geveth lif, feling, and resoun'. The poets sometimes allow
themselves to talk as if man had, not a three-storied soul,
but three souls. Donne, claiming that the Vegetable
Soul by which he grows, the Sensitive Soul by which he

[1] *Moralia*, VI, 16.   [2] Migne, CCX, 222[d].
[3] *R. de la Rose*, 19,043 *sq.*   [4] Prol. 945.

sees, and the Rational Soul by which he understands, are all equally delighted in the beloved, says,

> all my souls bee
> Emparadis'd in you (in Whom alone
> I understand, and grow, and see).
> (A Valediction of My Name, 25.)

But this is merely a trope. Donne knows he has only one soul, which, being Rational, includes the Sensitive and the Vegetable.

The Rational Soul is sometimes called simply 'Reason', and the Sensitive Soul simply 'Sensuality'. This is the sense of these words when the Parson in Chaucer says, 'God sholde have lordschipe over reson, and reson over sensualite, and sensualite over the body of man' (I. 262).

All three kinds of soul are immaterial. The soul—as we should say, the 'life'—of a tree or herb is not a part of it which could be found by dissection; nor is a man's Rational Soul in that sense a 'part' of the man. And all soul, like every other substance, is created by God. The peculiarity of Rational Soul is that it is created in each case by the immediate act of God, whereas other things mostly come into existence by developments and transmutations within the total created order.[1] Genesis ii. 7 is no doubt the source for this; but Plato had also set the creation of man apart from creation in general.[2]

The soul's turning to God is often treated in the poets as a returning and therefore one more instance of 'kindly

---

[1] On the whole question, see Aquinas Iª, XC, art. 2, 3.
[2] *Timaeus*, 41ᶜ *sq.*

enclyning'. Hence Chaucer's 'Repeireth *hoom* from worldly vanitee' in *Troilus*, v, 1837, or Deguileville's

> To Him of verray ryht certeyn
> Thou must resorte and tourne ageyn
> As by moeving natural.
> (*Pilgrimage*, trans. Lydgate, 12,262 *sq.*)

Such passages perhaps reflect nothing more than the doctrine of man's special and immediate creation by God; but it is hard to be sure. The doctrine of pre-existence (in some better world than this) was firmly rejected in the scholastic age. The 'inconvenience' of making the Rational Soul begin to exist only when the body begins to exist and also holding that it existed after the body's death, was palliated by the reminder that death—one of those 'two things that were never made'[1]—had no place in the original creation. It is not the soul's nature to leave the body; rather, the body (disnatured by the Fall) deserts the soul.[2] But in the Seminal Period and the earlier Middle Ages the Platonic belief that we had lived before we were incarnate on earth, still hung in the air. Chalcidius had preserved what Plato says about this in *Phaedrus* 245[a]. He had also preserved *Timaeus* 35[a] and 41[d]. These very difficult passages may not really imply the pre-existence of the individual soul, but they could easily be thought to do so. Origen held that all those souls which now animate human bodies were created at the same time as the angels and had long existed before their terrestrial birth. Even St Augustine, in a passage quoted by Aquinas,[3]

[1] Donne, *Litanie*, 10–11.   [2] See Aquinas, *loc. cit.* art 4.
[3] I[a], xc, art. 4.

entertains, subject to revision, the view that Adam's soul was already in existence while his body still 'slept in its causes'. The full Platonic doctrine seems to be implied—with what philosophic seriousness I do not know—by Bernardus Silvestris[1] when Noys sees in Heaven countless souls weeping because they will soon have to descend from that *splendor* into these glooms.

At the Renaissance the recovery of the Platonic *corpus* and the revival of Platonism re-awoke the doctrine. It is taken with full seriousness by Ficino and, later, by Henry More. Whether Spenser in the *Hymne of Beautie* (197 *sq.*) or in the Garden of Adonis (*F.Q.* III, vi, 33) has more than a poetic half-belief in it, may be doubted. Thomas Browne, not venturing on the doctrine, would gladly retain the flavour of it: 'though it looks but like an imaginary kind of existency to be before we are', yet to have pre-existed eternally in the divine foreknowledge 'is somewhat more than a non-entity' (*Christian Morals*). Vaughan's *Retreate* and even Wordsworth's *Ode* have been diversely interpreted. Only with the late nineteenth century and the Theosophists does pre-existence—now envisaged as the 'wisdom of the East'—recover a foot-hold in Europe.

D. RATIONAL SOUL

We have noticed that the term *angels* sometimes covers all the aetherial beings and is sometimes restricted to the lowest of their nine species. In the same way the word *reason* sometimes means Rational Soul, and sometimes

[1] *Op. cit.* II, *Pros.* iii, p. 37.

Earth and her Inhabitants

means the lower of the two faculties which Rational Soul exercises. These are *Intellectus* and *Ratio*.

Intellectus is the higher, so that if we call it 'understanding', the Coleridgean distinction which puts 'reason' above 'understanding' inverts the traditional order. Boethius, it will be remembered, distinguishes *intelligentia* from *ratio*; the former being enjoyed in its perfection by angels. *Intellectus* is that in man which approximates most nearly to angelic *intelligentia*; it is in fact *obumbrata intelligentia*, clouded intelligence, or a shadow of intelligence. Its relation to reason is thus described by Aquinas: 'intellect (*intelligere*) is the simple (i.e. indivisible, uncompounded) grasp of an intelligible truth, whereas reasoning (*ratiocinari*) is the progression towards an intelligible truth by going from one understood (*intellecto*) point to another. The difference between them is thus like the difference between rest and motion or between possession and acquisition' (I^a, LXXIX, art. 8). We are enjoying *intellectus* when we 'just see' a self-evident truth; we are exercising *ratio* when we proceed step by step to prove a truth which is not self-evident. A cognitive life in which all truth can be simply 'seen' would be the life of an *intelligentia*, an angel. A life of unmitigated *ratio* where nothing was simply 'seen' and all had to be proved, would presumably be impossible; for nothing can be proved if nothing is self-evident. Man's mental life is spent in laboriously connecting those frequent, but momentary, flashes of *intelligentia* which constitute *intellectus*.

When *ratio* is used with this precision and distinguished

Passim e Reason!

from *intellectus*, it is, I take it, very much what we mean by 'reason' today; that is, as Johnson defines it, 'The power by which man deduces one proposition from another, or proceeds from premises to consequences'. But, having so defined it, he gives as his first example, from Hooker, 'Reason is the director of man's will, discovering in action what is good'. There would seem to be a startling discrepancy between the example and the definition. No doubt, if A is good for its own sake, we may discover by reasoning that, since B is the means to A, therefore B would be a good thing to do. But by what sort of deduction, and from what sort of premises, could we reach the proposition 'A is good for its own sake'? This must be accepted from some other source before the reasoning can begin; a source which has been variously identified—with 'conscience' (conceived as the Voice of God), with some moral 'sense' or 'taste', with an emotion ('a good heart'), with the standards of one's social group, with the super-ego.

Yet nearly all moralists before the eighteenth century regarded Reason as the organ of morality. The moral conflict was depicted as one between Passion and Reason, not between Passion and 'conscience', or 'duty', or 'goodness'. Prospero, in forgiving his enemies, declares that he is siding, not with his charity or mercy, but with 'his nobler reason' (*Tempest*, v, i, 26). The explanation is that nearly all of them believed the fundamental moral maxims were intellectually grasped. If they had been using the strict medieval distinction, they would have made morality an affair not of *ratio* but of *intellectus*. This distinction, however, even in the Middle Ages, was used only by philosophers, and did not affect popular or poetic language. On that level *Reason* means Rational Soul. Moral imperatives therefore were uttered by Reason, though, in the stricter terminology, reasoning about moral questions doubtless received all her premises from Intellect—just as geometry is an affair of Reason, though it depends on axioms which cannot be reached by reasoning.

Johnson, in the passage quoted from his *Dictionary*, is for once confused. He wrote when the older ethical view was in rapid decline and the meaning of the word *reason* consequently in rapid change. The eighteenth century witnessed a revolt against the doctrine that moral judgements are wholly, or primarily, or at all, rational. Even Butler in the *Sermons* (1726) gave the role which had once been Reason's to 'Reflection or Conscience'. Others handed the normative function over to a moral 'sentiment' or 'taste'. In Fielding the source of good conduct is good feeling, and the claims of Reason to be that source are ridiculed in the person of Mr Square. Mackenzie's *Man of Feeling* (1771) carried this process further. In Wordsworth 'the heart' can be favourably contrasted with 'the head'. In some nineteenth-century fiction one particular system of feelings, the domestic affections, seem not only to inspire but to constitute morality. The linguistic result of this process was to narrow the meaning of the word *reason*. From meaning (in all but the most philosophical contexts) the whole Rational Soul, both *intellectus* and *ratio*, it shrank to meaning merely 'the power by which man deduces one proposition from another'. This change had begun in Johnson's time. He inadvertently defines the word in its newer and narrower sense, and immediately illustrates it in that which was older and larger.

The belief that to recognise a duty was to perceive a truth—not because you had a good heart but because you were an intellectual being—had roots in antiquity. Plato preserved the Socratic idea that morality was an affair of knowledge; bad men were bad because they did not know what was good. Aristotle, while attacking this view and giving an important place to upbringing and habituation, still made 'right reason' (ὀρθὸς λόγος) essential to good conduct. The Stoics believed in a Natural Law which all rational men, in virtue of their rationality, saw to be binding on them. St Paul has a curious function in this story. His statement in Romans (ii. 14 *sq.*) that there is a law 'written in the hearts' even of Gentiles who do not know 'the law', is in full conformity with the Stoic conception, and would for centuries be so understood. Nor, during those centuries, would the word *hearts* have had merely emotional associations. The Hebrew word which St Paul represents by καρδία would be more nearly translated 'Mind'; and in Latin, one who is *cordatus* is not a man of feeling but a man of sense. But later, when fewer people thought in Latin, and the new ethics of feeling were coming into fashion, this Pauline use of *hearts* may well have seemed to support the novelty.

The importance of all this for our own purpose is that nearly every reference to Reason in the old poets will be in some measure misread if we have in mind only 'the power by which man deduces one proposition from another'. One of the most moving passages in Guillaume de Lorris' part of the *Romance of the Rose* (5813 *sq.*) is that where Reason, Reason the beautiful, a gracious lady, a humbled goddess, deigns to plead with the lover as a celestial mistress, a rival to his earthly love. This is frigid if Reason were only what Johnson made her. You cannot turn a calculating machine into a goddess. But *Raison la bele* is 'no such cold thing'. She is not even Wordsworth's personified Duty; not even—though this brings us nearer—the personified virtue of Aristotle's ode, 'for whose virgin beauty men will die' (σᾶς πέρι, παρθένε, μορφᾶς). She is *intelligentia obumbrata*, the shadow of angelic nature in man. So again in Shakespeare's *Lucrece* we need to know fully who the 'spotted princess' (719–28) is: Tarquin's Reason, rightful sovereign of his soul, now maculate. Many references to Reason in *Paradise Lost* need the same gloss. It is true that we still have in our modern use of 'reasonable' a survival of the old sense, for when we complain that a selfish man is unreasonable we do not mean that he is guilty of a *non sequitur* or an undistributed middle. But it is far too humdrum and jejune to recall much of the old association.

E. SENSITIVE AND VEGETABLE SOUL

The Sensitive Soul has ten Senses or Wits, five of which are 'outward' and five 'inward'. The Outward Senses or Wits are what we call the Five Senses today: sight, hearing, smell, taste, and touch. Sometimes the inward five are called simply Wits, and the outward five simply Senses, as in Shakespeare's

> But my five wits nor my five senses can
> Dissuade one foolish heart from loving thee.
>
> > (*Sonnet* CXLI.)

The inward Wits are memory, estimation, imagination, phantasy, and common wit (or common sense). Of these, memory calls for no comment.

Estimation, or (*Vis*) *Aestimativa*, covers much of what is now covered by the word *instinct*. Albertus Magnus, whom I follow throughout this passage, tells us in his *De Anima* that it is Estimation which enables a cow to pick out her own calf from a crowd of calves or teaches an animal to fly from its natural enemy. Estimation detects the practical, the biological, significance of things, their *intentiones* (II, iv). Chaucer is referring to it, though not by name, when he says

> naturelly a beast desyreth flee
> Fro his contrarie if he may it see,
> Though he never erst had seyn it with his ye.
>
> > (*Nun's Priest's Tale*, B 4469.)

The distinction between Phantasy and Imagination—(*vis*) *phantastica* and (*vis*) *imaginativa*—is not so simple. Phantasy is the higher of the two; here Coleridge has once more turned the nomenclature upside down. To the best of my knowledge no medieval author mentions either faculty as a characteristic of poets. If they had been given to talking about poets in that way at all—they usually talk only of their language or their learning—

I think they would have used *invention* where we use *imagination*. According to Albertus, Imagination merely retains what has been perceived, and Phantasy deals with this *componendo et dividendo*, separating and uniting. I do not understand why *boni imaginativi* should tend, as he says they do, to be good at mathematics. Can this mean that paper was too precious to be wasted on rough figures and you geometrised, so far as possible, with figures merely held before the mind's eye? But I doubt it; there was always sand.

This psychological account of Phantasy and Imagination does not, in any case, cover popular usage in the vernacular. Albertus warns us that *Phantastica* is called *cogitativa* by the vulgar; that is, they say they are 'thinking' about something when in reality they are playing with mental images of it, *componendo et dividendo*. If he had known English he would probably have been interested to learn that in it an almost opposite fate had overtaken the word *imagination* (or *imaginatyf* which, as an ellipsis of *vis imaginativa*, often means the same thing). For in English *Imagination* meant, not merely the retention of things perceived, but 'having in mind' or 'thinking about', or 'taking into account' in the largest and loosest sense. Langland's Ymaginatyf, having explained that he is *vis imaginativa*, goes on to say

> idel was I nevere,
> And many times have moeved thee to think on thin ende.
> (*Piers Plowman*, B XII, 1.)

Whether the dreamer's end is his death or his lot in the next world, it is certainly not something of which he had any percepts to retain. Ymaginatyf means 'I have often reminded you that you must die'. So in Berners' Froissart: 'King Peter, seeing himself thus beset round with his enemies, was in great imagination' (I, 242); that is, he had plenty on his mind. Chaucer says of Arveragus, coming home to his wife,

> Nothing list him to been imaginatyf
> If any wight had spoke, whil he was oute,
> To hire of love. (*Franklin's Tale*, F 1094.)

No doubt the activity which Arveragus abstained from, like that which was forced upon King Peter, would be accompanied by what we call imagination, and plenty of it. But I do not think either writer has that especially in view. Chaucer means that Arveragus wasn't one 'to get ideas into his head'.

Common Sense (or Wit) as a term in medieval psychology must not be confused either with *communis sensus* (the common opinion of mankind) or with 'common sense' as gumption or elementary rationality—a much later usage. Albertus gives it two functions: (*a*) 'It judges of the operation of a sense so that when we see, we know we are seeing'; (*b*) it puts together the data given by the five senses, or Outward Wits, so that we can say an orange is sweet or one orange is sweeter than another. Burton, centuries later, says 'this common sense is the judge or moderator of the rest, by whom we discern all differences of objects; for by mine eye I do not know that I see, or by mine ear that I hear, but by my common sense'.[1] Common sense is that which turns mere sensa-

[1] Pt. I, i, M 2, subs. 7.

tions into coherent consciousness of myself as subject in a world of objects. It is very close to what some call Apperception and what Coleridge called Primary Imagination. The difficulty of becoming aware of it arises from the fact that we are never without it except in states which cannot, for that very reason, be fully remembered. Partial anaesthesia, when we have sentience without full consciousness, is one of them. Sidney describes another in the *Arcadia* when he says that two knights in the heat of battle could ignore their gashes, 'wrath and courage barring the common sense from bringing any message of their case to the mind' (1590, III, 18).

There is no need to write a separate section on the Vegetable Soul. It is responsible for all the unconscious, involuntary processes in our organism: for growth, secretion, nutrition, and reproduction. As regards the two last, this does not mean that eating or sexual intercourse is unconscious or involuntary. It is the unconscious and involuntary processes set up by these acts which belong to Vegetable Soul.

F. SOUL AND BODY

No Model yet devised has made a satisfactory unity between our actual experience of sensation or thought or emotion and any available account of the corporeal processes which they are held to involve. We experience, say, a chain of reasoning; thoughts, which are 'about' or 'refer to' something other than themselves, are linked together by the logical relation of grounds and consequents. Physiology resolves this into a sequence of cerebral events. But physical events, as such, cannot in any intelligible sense be said to be 'about' or to 'refer to' anything. And they must be linked to one another not as grounds and consequents but as causes and effects—a relation so irrelevant to the logical linkage that it is just as perfectly illustrated by the sequence of a maniac's thoughts as by the sequence of a rational man's. The chasm between the two points of view is so abrupt that desperate remedies have been adopted. Berkeleyan idealists have denied the physical process; extreme Behaviourists, the mental.

This perennial problem presented itself to the medieval thinker in two forms.

(1) How can the soul, conceived as an immaterial substance, act upon matter at all? Obviously it cannot act as one body acts upon another. Whether this way of putting the question differs at bottom from the way I have put it in the preceding paragraph might be debated.

(2) 'It is not possible to passe from one extreme to another but by a meane.'[1] This is the old maxim from *Timaeus* 31^{b-c} which so multiplied Triads in Apuleius, Chalcidius, pseudo-Dionysius, and Alanus. This deep-seated principle would probably have moved the medievals to put something in between soul and body even if the psycho-physical question did not in all periods offer us the raw edge that I have indicated. And this principle made it certain in advance that their method of coping with the raw edge would be to supply a *tertium quid*.

This *tertium quid*, this phantom liaison-officer between body and soul, was called *Spirit* or (more often) the

[1] Bright (see J. Winny, *The Frame of Order*, 1957, p. 57).

spirits. It must be understood that this sense does not at all overlap with the sense which enables us to speak of angels or devils or ghosts as 'spirits'. To pass from the one meaning to the other would be merely to make a pun.

The spirits were supposed to be just sufficiently material for them to act upon the body, but so very fine and attenuated that they could be acted upon by the wholly immaterial soul. They were, putting it bluntly, to be like the aether of nineteenth-century physics, which, for all I could ever learn of it, was to be and not to be matter. This doctrine of the spirits seems to me the least reputable feature in the Medieval Model. If the *tertium quid* is matter at all (what have density and rarity to do with it?) both ends of the bridge rest on one side of the chasm; if not, both rest on the other.

Spirits, then, are the 'subtle *gumphus*'[1] required by Plato and Alanus to keep body and soul together, or as Donne says, 'the subtile knot which makes us man'.[2] They arise—we still speak of our spirits rising—from the blood like an exhalation; in Milton's language 'like gentle breaths from rivers pure' (*Paradise Lost*, IV, 804). Bartholomaeus Anglicus in the *De Proprietatibus* (thirteenth century), Englished by Trevisa, gives the following account of them. From blood, seething in the liver, there arises a 'smoke'. This, being 'pured', becomes Natural Spirit, which moves the blood and 'sendeth it about into all the limbs'. Entering the head, this Natural Spirit undergoes a further refinement—is 'more pured'—and so turns into Vital Spirit, which 'worketh in the artery veins the pulses

[1] See above, p. 60. [2] *Extasie*, 61.

of life'. Some of it enters the brain where it is once more 'made subtle' and becomes Animal Spirit. Of this, some is distributed to the 'limbs of feeling' (the organs of sensation); some remains in the 'dens' of the brain to serve as the vehicle of the Inward Wits; flowing out at the back of the skull into the spinal marrow, it provides for voluntary movement (III, xxii). This Animal Spirit is the immediate organ of the Rational Soul through which alone she acts when incarnate. 'We may not believe', adds Bartholomaeus, 'that this spirit is man's reasonable soul, but more soothly, as saith Austin, the car thereof and proper instrument. For by means of such a spirit the soul is joined to the body.' For Bartholomaeus' triad of Natural, Vital, and Animal Spirits, other accounts substitute Vital, Animal, and Intellectual.[1] But, however classified, the Spirits have always the same function. As Timothy Bright says in his *Treatise of Melancholy*[2] (1586), they are 'a true love knot to couple heaven and earth together; yea, a more divine nature than the heavens with a base clod of earth', so that the soul is 'not fettered with the bodie, as certaine Philosophers have taken it, but handfasted therewith by that golden claspe of the spirit'.

The Spirits also enable us to give an account of insanity without having to say—which would have been felt as a contradiction in terms—that Rational Soul herself can lose her rationality. As Bartholomaeus says in the same place, when the Spirits are impaired, the 'accord' of body and soul is resolved, so that the Rational Soul 'is let' (hindered, of all its 'works in the body, as it is seen in

---

[1] Cf. *Paradise Lost*, v, 483 *sq.*   [2] Winny, *op. cit.* pp. 57–8.

them that be amazed, and mad men and frantic'. The appropriate Spirit being out of order, Rational Soul has no purchase on the material body.

Intellectuales spiritus, Intellectual Spirits, can by ellipsis become 'intellectuals' and even, presumably by confusion, 'intellects'. Hence Johnson in *Rambler*, 95, speaks of a man's 'intellects' being 'disturbed', or Lamb writes 'your fear for Hartley's intellectuals is just'.[1]

We have seen from Bartholomaeus that the Spirits can be localised in different parts of the body. Hence it is not unreasonable that some of the functions which the soul exercises by means of them can also be localised. In the passage I have already quoted he assigns Common Wit and 'the virtue imaginative' to the 'foremost den' or frontal cavity of the head, understanding to the 'middle den', and memory to the hindmost. Readers of the *Faerie Queene* will remember that Spenser, though omitting Common Wit, similarly locates imagination (Phantastes) in the front, reason in the middle, and memory at the back (II, ix, 44 *sq.*). It is to this central 'den' that Lady Macbeth refers when she speaks of the 'receipt (receptacle) of reason' (I, vii, 66).

G. THE HUMAN BODY

The human body gives us another sense in which man can be called a microcosm, for it, like the world, is built out of the four contraries. In the great world, it will be remembered, these combine to form the elements—fire, air, water, earth. But in our bodies they combine to form the

[1] To Southey, 8 Aug. 1815.

Humours. Hot and Moist make Blood; Hot and Dry, Choler; Cold and Moist, Phlegm; Cold and Dry, Melancholy. Popular language, however, does not always observe the distinction between Humours made of Contraries within us and Elements made of Contraries without us. When Marlowe in *Tamburlaine* (869) says 'Nature that fram'd us of four elements' or Shakespeare speaks of the 'elements' being perfectly mixed in Brutus (*Julius Caesar*, v, v, 73), they are using 'elements' to mean either Humours or Contraries.

The proportion in which the Humours are blended differs from one man to another and constitutes his *complexio* or *temperamentum*, his combination or mixture. This explains the odd fact that in modern English 'to lose one's temper' and 'to show one's temper' are synonymous expressions. If you have a good *temperamentum* you may momentarily lose it when you are angry. If you have a bad one, you may 'show it' when anger puts you off your guard. For the same reason a man who is often angry has a bad *temperamentum* or is 'ill-tempered'. Such expressions led careless speakers to think that *temper* meant simply anger, and this finally became its commonest sense. But so much of the old usage survives that flying 'into' a temper and being put 'out of' temper now co-exist as synonyms.

Though the proportion of the Humours is perhaps never exactly the same in any two individuals, the complexions can obviously be grouped into four main types according to the Humour that predominates in each. One of the symptoms of a man's complexion is his colouring; that is, his 'complexion' in the modern sense. But I do not think the word ever had that sense in Middle English. Their word for what we call 'complexion' was *rode*; as in the *Miller's Tale*, 'his rode was reed, his eyen greye as goos' (A 3317).

Where Blood predominates we have the Sanguine Complexion. This is the best of the four, for Blood is especially 'natures friend' (*Squire's Tale*, F 353). Sir Thomas Elyot in his *Castle of Health* (1534) enumerates as the signs of the Sanguine man 'visage white and ruddy ...sleep much...dremes of blouddy things or things pleasant...angry shortly'. The dreams, I take it, are not of wounds and strife so much as of blood-red colours. The 'pleasant' things are what we should call 'merry'. The Sanguine man's anger is easily roused but short-lived; he is a trifle peppery, but not sullen or vindictive. Chaucer's Franklin, a text-book case of this Complexion, could give his cook a sound rating,[1] but he had obviously a good heart. Shakespeare's Beatrice—she too could be 'angry shortly'—was probably Sanguine. The Sanguine man is plump, cheerful, and hopeful. A fifteenth-century manuscript[2] symbolises this complexion by a man and a woman richly dressed, playing on stringed instruments in a flowery place.

The Choleric man is tall and lean. Chaucer's Reeve was 'a sclendre colerik man', and his legs were 'ful longe... and ful lene' (A 587 *sq.*). Like the Sanguine, he is easily moved to anger; so that Chantecleer, who suffers from a 'superfluitee...of rede colera' (B 5117–18), will even

[1] A 351. [2] Brit. Mus. Add. 17,987.

start a quarrel with laxatives in general—'I hem defye, I love hem nevere a del' (B 4348). But, unlike the Sanguine, the Choleric are vindictive. The Reeve pays the Miller out for his story, and the peasants on his own manor feared him as they feared death (A 605). Cholerics dream of thunder and of bright, dangerous things, like arrows and fire, as Peretelote knows (B 4120). The same manuscript that I mentioned above shows, for its symbol of the Choleric Complexion, a man holding a woman by the hair and beating her with a club. Choleric children are now described (by their mothers) as 'highly strung'.

Elyot's symptoms of the Melancholy Complexion run: 'leane...moche watch (i.e. he is a bad sleeper)...dreames fearful...stiff in opinions...anger long and fretting'. Hamlet diagnoses himself as melancholy (II, ii, 640), refers to his bad dreams[1] (*ibid.* 264), and is an extreme example of 'anger long and fretting'. He may be lean too; for 'fat' in v, ii, 298 probably means 'all in a muck sweat'. Today I think we should describe the Melancholy man as a neurotic. I mean, the Melancholy man of the Middle Ages. The sense of the word melancholy was changing in the sixteenth century and began often to mean either simply 'sad' or else 'reflective, thoughtful, introverted'. Thus in the poem prefixed to Burton's *Anatomy* 'melancholy' seems to be simply reverie, endlessly indulged in solitude, with all its pains but also with all its pleasures, the waking dreams of fear-fulfilment and wish-fulfilment alike. In Dürer's picture

---

[1] Enigmatically, to be sure. But they support the Melancholy *atmosphere.*

Malencolia is apparently the studious, withdrawn, and meditative life.

The Phlegmatic is perhaps the worst of all the Complexions. Elyot gives as the signs of it 'fatnesse...colour white...sleepe superfluous (i.e. in excess)...dremes of things watery or of fish...slownesse...dulnesse of lerning...smallness of courage'. The Phlegmatic boy or girl, fat, pale, sluggish, dull, is the despair of parents and teachers; by others, either made a butt or simply unnoticed. The text-book case is the first Mrs Milton, if, as we suspect, her husband was thinking of her when in the *Doctrine and Discipline* he commiserated the man who 'shall find himself bound fast...to an image of earth and phlegm' (I, 5). Mary Bennet in *Pride and Prejudice* was probably a Phlegmatic.

Like the Planets, the Complexions need to be lived with imaginatively, not merely learned as concepts. They do not exactly correspond to any psychological classification we have been taught to make. But most of those we know (except ourselves) will illustrate one or other of the four tolerably well.

In addition to this permanent predominance of some one Humour in each individual, there is also a daily rhythmic variation which gives each of the four a temporary predominance in all of us. Blood is dominant from midnight till 6 a.m.; Choler, from then till noon; Melancholy, from noon till 6 p.m.; then Phlegm till midnight. (All this, it should be remembered, is geared for people who got up and went to bed far earlier than we.) Sleep, in the *Squire's Tale*, warned people to go to bed at the right time 'for blood was in his dominacioun' (F 347). The technical term *domination* can be jokingly extended to things other than Humours, as when the Manciple says of the Cook 'drink hath dominacioun upon this man' (H 57). This small witticism is often lost on modern readers.

H. THE HUMAN PAST

It has sometimes been said that Christianity inherited from Judaism and imposed on the Western world a new conception of history. To the Greeks, we are told, the historical process was a meaningless flux or cyclic reiteration. Significance was to be sought not in the world of becoming but in that of being, not in history but in metaphysics, mathematics, and theology. Hence Greek historians wrote of such past actions—the Persian or the Peloponnesian War, or the lives of great men—as have a unity in themselves, and were seldom curious to trace from its beginnings the development of a people or a state. History, in a word, was not for them a story with a plot. The Hebrews, on the other hand, saw their whole past as a revelation of the purposes of Jahweh. Christianity, going on from there, makes world-history in its entirety a single, transcendentally significant, story with a well-defined plot pivoted on Creation, Fall, Redemption, and Judgement.

On this view the *differentia* of Christian historiography ought to be what I call Historicism; the belief that by studying the past we can learn not only historical but meta-historical or transcendental truth. When Novalis called history 'an evangel', when Hegel saw in it the progressive self-manifestation of absolute spirit, when Carlyle spoke of it as 'a book of revelations', they were Historicists. Keats's Oceanus speaks as a Historicist when he claims to discern an

> eternal law
> That first in beauty should be first in might.

In reality, the best medieval historians, like the best historians in other periods, are seldom Historicists.

The suggested antithesis between Pagan and Christian conceptions of history is certainly overdrawn. Not all Pagans were Greeks. The Norse gods, unlike the Olympians, are continuously involved in a tragic and tragically significant temporal process. Eddaic theology, no less than Hebraic, makes cosmic history a story with a plot; an irreversible story marching deathward to the drumbeat of omens and prophecies. Nor were the Romans much less inveterate Historicists than the Jews. How Rome came to be and to be great was the theme of most historians and of all pre-Virgilian epic. What Virgil puts forward in a mythical form is precisely meta-history. The whole mundane process, the *fata Jovis*, are in labour to bring forth the endless and dedicated empire of Rome.

Christian Historicism also exists; as in St Augustine's *De Civitate Dei*, Orosius' *History against the Pagans*, or Dante's *De Monarchia*. But the two first were written to answer, and the third to baptise, a Pagan Historicism which was already in existence. The elementary Historicism which sees divine judgements in all disasters—the beaten side always deserved their beating—or the still more elementary sort which holds that everything is, and always was, going to the dogs—is not uncommon. Wulfstan's *sermo ad Anglos* illustrates both. Some German historians in the twelfth century are Historicists of a more thorough-going kind. The extreme example is Joachim of Flora (*ob.* 1202). But he was not a Historian; rather, as was said, 'a dabbler in the future'[1]—it is, indeed, that period in which radical Historicists often feel most at home. But the chroniclers who have contributed most to our knowledge of medieval history, or who have proved the most permanently attractive, were not of this kind.

No doubt all history in the last resort must be held by Christians to be a story with a divine plot. But not all Christian historiographers feel it their business to take much notice of that. For it is, as known to men, only an overall plot, like the rise and fall of Arthur in Malory or the loves of Roger and Bradamant in Ariosto. Like them, it is festooned with a huge wealth of subordinate stories, each of which has itself a beginning, a middle, and an end, but which do not in the aggregate display any single trend in the world depicted. These can be told for their own sake. They need not, perhaps cannot, be related to the central theological story of the human race. Indeed, the medieval conception of Fortune tends to discourage attempts at a 'philosophy of history'. If most events happen because Fortune is turning her wheel, 'rejoicing in her bliss', and giving everyone his turn, the ground is cut from under the feet of a Hegel, a Carlyle, a

[1] F. Heer, *The Medieval World*, trans. J. Sandheimer (1961).

Spengler, a Marxist, and even a Macaulay. As W. P. Ker said, 'The interest of history was too great and varied to be ruled by the formulas of Orosius; the chroniclers generally find their own points of view, and these in many cases, fortunately, are not those of the preacher'.[1]

Medieval historians, even when we have ruled out the radical Historicists, are a mixed collection. Some of them —Matthew Paris, for example, and perhaps Snorre— have the scientific approach and are critical of their sources. But they are not on that account especially important for our present purpose. We are concerned with the picture of the past, and the attitude to the past, as these existed in the mind of literary authors and their audience. The imagined past as part of the Model is the quarry we pursue.

John Barbour (*ob.* 1395) at the beginning of his *Bruce* sets out what he thinks the true reasons for studying history. Stories, even when untrue, give pleasure. But, if so, true stories well told ('said on gud maner'), ought to give a double pleasure; pleasure in the 'carpyng', the narrative as such, and pleasure in learning what really happened ('the thing rycht as it wes'). And thirdly, it is only fair to record the deeds of great men, for they deserve fame—'suld weill have prys' (I, 1–36). Historiography has then three functions: to entertain our imagination, to gratify our curiosity, and to discharge a debt we owe our ancestors. Joinville's Chronicle of St Louis, being a saint's life, concentrates on the third function—it is written 'in honour of this true saint'—but also fulfils the other two. Froissart (I, Prol.) approaches his work in much the same

[1] *The Dark Ages* (1923), p. 41.

spirit as Barbour. He writes in order that 'honourable and noble adventures of feats of arms...should notably be enregistered and put in perpetual memory'. And such a record will give 'pastance' and 'pleasure'. He adds—a point omitted by Barbour—that it will also furnish 'ensample'. By this he does not mean those 'lessons of history' which can be drawn from the success or failure of previous statesmanship or strategy. He means that by reading of valiant deeds 'the prewe and hardy may have ensample to encourage them'.

It is to be noticed that the approach we find in these historians differs not at all from that of authors whose matter we regard as wholly legendary. The author of the fourteenth-century Troy book, the *Geste Hystoriale*, begins very much as Barbour does. He writes to preserve the 'aunters' of noble ancestors which are now 'almost out of mind'. He hopes that 'old stories of brave men who were in high place may be a *solas*' to those who learn them from writers who knew the fact at first hand (*wist it in dede*). He goes on to enumerate his sources, explaining why Homer is unreliable. Lydgate in his *Troy Book* (1412) says that great *conquerouris* would by now have lost their due fame if reliable *auctours*, whom he is using, had not preserved for us 'the verrie trewe corn' of fact separated from the chaff of fiction,

> For in her hand they hilde for a staf
> The trouthe only. (*Prologue*, 152.)

They could not have been flatterers, for they wrote after the death of the heroes whom they celebrated, and no one flatters the dead (184 *sq.*). Even Caxton, it will be remembered, though leaving us free to doubt some things in the prose *Morte*, professes to have been convinced by argument of Arthur's historicity. And his emphasis on the 'exemplary' value of the book might, as we have seen, stand on the first page of any chronicle.

In more sophisticated ages we are familiar with the grave quasi-factual devices which some authors use to bestow verisimilitude on narratives which everyone knows for fiction; the sober mendacities of Defoe or Swift, the polyglot array of documents at the beginning of *She*. But I cannot believe that the medieval authors were playing that game. The very words *story* and *history* had not yet been desynonymised. Even Elizabethan chroniclers still begin the history of our island with Brut and his Trojans.

It follows that the distinction between history and fiction cannot, in its modern clarity, be applied to medieval books or to the spirit in which they were read. It is by no means necessary to suppose that Chaucer's contemporaries believed the tale of Troy or Thebes as we believe in the Napoleonic Wars; but neither did they disbelieve them as we disbelieve a novel.

Two passages, one from the father of history and one from Milton, who was perhaps the last historian of the old kind, seem to me to throw light on the question. 'It is my duty', says Herodotus, 'to record what has been told, but not always to believe it. This applies to my whole book' (VII, 152). Now Milton, in his *History of*

Britain[1] (the italics are mine): 'That which hath received approbation from so many, I have chosen not to omit. Certain or uncertain, be that upon the credit of those whom I must follow; so far as keeps aloof from impossible and absurd, attested by ancient writers from books more ancient, I refuse not, as *the due and proper subject of story*.'

Herodotus and Milton both disclaim any fundamental responsibility: if the earlier *auctours* have lied, on their own head be it. We may indeed expurgate the 'impossible and absurd'. But this does not mean what will be found absurd after considering all the evidence afresh as if one were the first explorer, as if no 'story' had been already established. It means what is *prima facie* absurd by the standards of one's own age. Chaucer may well have believed all the miracles in Nicholas Trivet's story of Constance; what struck him as absurd was that a sensible man like Alla would have committed such a *faux pas* as to make a child his messenger to the Emperor. Accordingly, he corrects it (B 1086–92). But the italicised words are the really illuminating ones. So far from having failed in his duty by handing on the existing 'story' (with minor expurgations) instead of producing a new and better grounded 'story' of his own, the historian has done what historians are there to do. For precisely this is 'the true and proper subject of story'. This is what history is for. The medieval purchaser of a manuscript which purported to give the British or Trojan story did not want some individual clerk's opinions about the past, presump-

[1] Prose works (Bohn), vol. v, p. 168.

tuously setting themselves up against what 'hath received approbation from many'. At that rate there would soon be as many versions of the story as there were chroniclers. He wanted (as Milton thinks he is entitled to have) the established Model of the past; tinkered a little here and there, but substantially the same. This was what was useful—for conversation, for poets, for 'ensamples'.

I am inclined to think that most of those who read 'historial' works about Troy, Alexander, Arthur, or Charlemagne, believed their matter to be in the main true. But I feel much more certain that they did not believe it to be false. I feel surest of all that the question of belief or disbelief was seldom uppermost in their minds. That, if it was anyone's business, was not theirs. Their business was to learn the story. If its veracity were questioned they would feel that the burden of disproof lay wholly with the critic. Till that moment arrived (and it did not arrive often) the story had, by long prescription, a status in the common imagination indistinguishable—at any rate, not distinguished—from that of fact. Everyone 'knew'—as we all 'know' how the ostrich hides her head in the sand—that the past contained Nine Worthies: three Pagans (Hector, Alexander, and Julius Caesar); three Jews (Joshua, David, and Judas Maccabaeus); and three Christians (Arthur, Charlemagne, and Godfrey of Bouillon). Everyone 'knew' we were descended from the Trojans— as we all 'know' how Alfred burned the cakes and Nelson put the telescope to his blind eye. As the spaces above us were filled with daemons, angels, influences, and intelligences, so the centuries behind us were filled with

shining and ordered figures, with the deeds of Hector and
Roland, with the splendours of Charlemagne, Arthur,
Priam, and Solomon.

It must be remembered throughout that the texts we
should now call historical differed in outlook and narrative texture from those we should call fictions far less than
a modern 'history' differs from a modern novel. Medieval historians dealt hardly at all with the impersonal.
Social or economic conditions and national characteristics
come in only by accident or when they are required to
explain something in the narrative. The chronicles, like
the legends, are about individuals; their valour or villainy,
their memorable sayings, their good or bad luck. Hence
a modern finds those of the Dark Ages suspiciously epic
and those of the High Middle Ages suspiciously romantic.
Perhaps the suspicion is not always justified. The elements
of epic and romance, like those of economic and social
history, exist at all times in the real world; and historians,
even in dealing with contemporary events, will pick out
those elements which the habitual bent of their imagination has conditioned them to notice. Perhaps past or
future ages might wonder at the predominance of the
impersonal in some modern histories; might even ask,
'But were there no *people* at that time?' Even the turns
of expression may be the same in chronicle and romance.
Or dit le conte ('now tells the tale') will be found in
Froissart (I, iv).

All medieval narratives about the past are equally
lacking in the sense of period. For us the past is, before all
else, a 'costume play'. From our earliest picture-books

we learn the difference in clothes, weapons, furniture and architecture. We cannot remember in our lives any historical knowledge earlier than this. This superficial (and often inaccurate) characterisation of different ages helps far more than we suspect towards our later and subtler discriminations between them. It is difficult to think ourselves back into the minds of men for whom it did not exist. And in the Middle Ages, and long after, it did not. It was known that Adam went naked till he fell. After that, they pictured the whole past in terms of their own age. So indeed did the Elizabethans. So did Milton; he never doubted that 'capon and white broth' would have been as familiar to Christ and the disciples as to himself.[1] It is doubtful whether the sense of period is much older than the Waverley novels. It is hardly present in Gibbon. Walpole's *Otranto*, which would not now deceive school-children, could hope, not quite vainly, to deceive the public of 1765. Where even the most obvious and superficial distinctions between one century (or millennium) and another were ignored, the profounder differences of temper and mental climate were naturally not dreamed of. Authors may profess to know that things in Arthur's day or Hector's were not quite as in their own time, but the picture they actually paint belies the profession. Chaucer in a flash of astonishing insight acknowledges that in old Troy the language and procedure of courtship may have differed from those of his own day (*Troilus*, II, 22 *sq.*). But it is only a flash; momentary. The manners, the fighting, the religious services, the very traffic-

[1] *Smectymnuus*, Prose works (Bohn), vol. III, p. 127.

regulations of his Trojans, are fourteenth-century. It was this happy ignorance that gave the medieval carver or poet his power of touching into vivid life every 'historial' matter he took in hand. It also helped to exclude Historicism. For us, areas of the past are qualitatively distinguished. Anachronisms are therefore not merely errors; they offend like discords in music or inappropriate flavours in a dish. But when Isidore, at the threshold of the Middle Ages, divides all history into six *aetates* (v, xxxix) there is nothing qualitative about them. They are not phases in an evolution or acts in a drama; they are merely convenient chronological blocks. They tempt him to no speculation about the future. Having brought the sixth *aetas* down to his own time, he ends with the statement that the remainder of this *aetas* is known only to God.

The nearest we get to a widespread 'philosophy of history' in the Middle Ages is, as I have said, the frequent assertion that things were once better than they are now. As we read in Wulfstan's sermon: 'The world hurries on (*is on ofste*)...and speeds to its end...thus, for men's sins it must worsen day by day.' It was long ago, said Gower, that the world stood 'in all his welthe' (Prologue, 95). Love is not now as it was in Arthur's time, said Chrétien in the opening lines of *Yvain*. Malory agreed (XVIII, 25). Yet I do not find that in reading either chronicle or romance we really get an impression of gloom. The emphasis usually falls on the past splendour rather than on the subsequent decline. Medieval and nineteenth-century man agreed that their present was no very admirable age; not to be compared (said one) with the glory that was, not to be compared (said the other) with the glory that is still to come. The odd thing is that the first view seems to have bred on the whole a more cheerful temper. Historically as well as cosmically, medieval man stood at the foot of a stairway; looking up, he felt delight. The backward, like the upward, glance exhilarated him with a majestic spectacle, and humility was rewarded with the pleasures of admiration. And, thanks to his deficiency in the sense of period, that packed and gorgeous past was far more immediate to him than the dark and bestial past could ever be to a Lecky or a Wells. It differed from the present only by being better. Hector was like any other knight, only braver. The saints looked down on one's spiritual life, the kings, sages, and warriors on one's secular life, the great lovers of old on one's own amours, to foster, encourage, and instruct. There were friends, ancestors, patrons in every age. One had one's place, however modest, in a great succession; one need be neither proud nor lonely.

I. THE SEVEN LIBERAL ARTS

To give an educational curriculum a place in the Model of the universe may at first seem an absurdity; and it would be an absurdity if the medievals had felt about it as we feel about the 'subjects' in a syllabus today. But the syllabus was regarded as immutable;[1] the number seven is numinous; the Liberal Arts, by long prescription, had

[1] The actual practice, and history, of medieval education are a different matter. The relevant chapters of D. Knowles' *Evolution of Medieval Thought* (1962) are a good introduction.

achieved a status not unlike that of nature herself. The Arts, no less than the Virtues and Vices, were personified. Grammar, with her birch, still sits looking down on the cloisters of Magdalen. Dante in the *Convivio* most carefully mortises the Arts into the cosmic framework. Rhetoric, for example, corresponds to Venus; for one reason, because she is 'the loveliest of all other disciplines', *soavissima di tutte le altre scienze*. Arithmetic is like Sol; for as he gives light to all the other stars so she gives light to all other sciences, and as our eyes are dazzled by his light so our intelligence is baffled by the infinity of numbers. And so of the rest (II, xiii).

Everyone knows that the Arts are Grammar, Dialectic, Rhetoric, Arithmetic, Music, Geometry, and Astronomy. And almost everyone has met the mnemonic couplet

> Gram loquitur, Dia verba docet, Rhet verba colorat,
> Mus canit, Ar numerat, Geo ponderat, Ast colit astra.

The first three constitute the *Trivium* or threefold way; the last four, the *Quadrivium*.

'Grammar talks', as the couplet says; or, as Isidore defines her, 'Grammar is the skill of speech' (I, i). That is, she teaches us Latin. But we must not imagine that to learn grammar merely corresponded to what we should now call having a 'classical' education, or even to becoming a 'Humanist' in the Renaissance sense. Latin was still the living Esperanto of the western world and great works were still being written in it. It was the language *par excellence*, so that the very word Latin—*læden* in Anglo-Saxon and *leden* in Middle English—came to mean *language*. Canace in the *Squire's Tale* by means of her magic ring

> understood wel everything
> That any foul may in his ledene seyn.   (F 435.)

Italian *Latino* is used by Petrarch in the same sense. An interpreter is a *Latiner*, whence the name Latimer. But while Grammar was thus restricted to a single tongue, in another way it sometimes extended far beyond the realm it claims today. It had done so for centuries. Quintilian suggests *literatura* as the proper translation of Greek *grammatike* (II, i), and *literatura*, though it does not mean 'literature', included a good deal more than literacy. It included all that is required for 'making up' a 'set book': syntax, etymology, prosody, and the explanation of allusions. Isidore makes even history a department of Grammar (I, xli-xliv). He would have described the book I am now writing as a book of Grammar. *Scholarship* is perhaps our nearest equivalent. In popular usage *Grammatica* or *Grammaria* slid into the vague sense of learning in general; and since learning is usually an object both of respect and suspicion to the masses, grammar, in the form *grammary* comes to mean magic. Thus in the ballad of *King Estmere*, 'My mother was a western woman learned in grammarye'. And from *grammary*, by a familiar sound-change, comes *glamour*—a word whose associations with grammar and even with magic have now been annihilated by the beauty-specialists.

The invention of this art was traditionally ascribed to Carmente or Carmentis,[1] the daughter of King Evander.

[1] Isidore, I, iv; Gower, IV, 2637.

The real authorities were Aelius Donatus (fourth century) and Priscianus (fifth and sixth). One's well-thumbed manuscript of Donatus was one's *donat* or *donet*, which by an easy transference comes to mean the 'primer' or 'rudiments' of any subject whatever. Covetyse in *Piers Plowman* says 'ich drow me among drapers my donet to lerne'—my first steps in sharp practice (C VII, 215).

Dialectic in the couplet 'teaches words'; an obscure saying. What is really meant is that, having learned from grammar how to talk, we must learn from Dialectic how to talk sense, to argue, to prove and disprove. The medieval foundation of this art was at first an *Isagoge* or Introduction to Aristotle written by Porphyry and translated into Latin by Boethius. This is in intention merely a work on Logic. But everyone who has tried to teach mere Logic knows how difficult it is, especially with an intelligent pupil, to avoid raising questions which force us into metaphysics. Porphyry's little treatise raises them too and, in accordance with its limited purpose, leaves them unsolved. This methodological limitation was mistaken for a state of doubt, and the doubt was then attributed not to Porphyry but to Boethius. Hence the rhyme:

> Assidet Boethius stupens de hac lite,
> Audiens quid hic et hic asserat perite,
> Et quid cui faveat non discernit rite;
> Non praesumit solvere litem definite.[1]

---

[1] By them sits Boethius, lost in hesitation. Hearing upon either hand learn'd asseveration, Wondering which side to take in this disputation; So he durs'n't bring the case to a termination.

Two warnings may be useful to some; others, I hope, will pardon them.

(1) 'Dialectic' in the modern Marxist sense is here a red herring—Hegelian in origin. It must be completely set aside when we speak of ancient or medieval Dialectic. This means simply the art of disputation. It has nothing to do with the dynamic of history.

(2) Dialectic is concerned with proving. In the Middle Ages there are three kinds of proof; from Reason, from Authority, and from Experience. We establish a geometrical truth by Reason; a historical truth, by Authority, by *auctours*. We learn by experience that oysters do or do not agree with us. But the words which Middle English uses to express this trichotomy might sometimes deceive us. Often they are clear enough, as when the Wife of Bath says

> Experience, though noun auctoritee
> Were in this world, were right ynough to me
> To speke of wo that is in marriage.   (D 1.)

But unfortunately the word *experience* is not always used for the third type of proof. The variants are two. To learn by experience may be to *feel*; or, more misleading, knowledge by experience may be *preve* (that is, proof). Thus Chaucer opens his *Legend of Phillis* by saying that the maxim 'wikked frute cometh of a wikked tree' can be learned not only from authority but 'by preve'; that is, empirically. In the *Hous of Fame* the eagle says that the poet can 'fele' the theory of sound which he has just enunciated (826). In the *Knight's Tale* the line 'Ne who most felingly speketh of love' (A 2203) sounds very modern. But to 'speak feelingly' probably means to speak from first-hand experience. No doubt those who did so might also be expected to speak 'with most feeling' in our sense; but lexically, I question whether *felingly* in Middle English could mean 'emotionally'.

Everything that we should now call criticism belonged either to Grammar or to Rhetoric. The Grammarian explained a poet's metre and allusions: the Rhetorician dealt with structure and style. Neither had anything to say about the point of view or the individual sensibility, the majesty or piquancy or pathos or humour, which structure and style embody. Hence poets are nearly always praised on purely stylistic grounds. Virgil is for Dante the poet who taught him his *bello stilo* (*Inferno*, I, 86). Petrarch in the *Clerk's Prologue* is for Chaucer the man who illuminated all Italy with his 'rethoryke swete' (E 31). Chaucer in the *Book of Thebes* is for Lydgate the 'flour' of poets in Britain by his 'excellence in rethorike and in eloquence' (Prologue, 40). All Chaucer's medieval successors speak of him in this way. You could not discover from their eulogies that he had ever presented a lifelike character or told a merry tale.

The ancient teachers of Rhetoric addressed their precepts to orators in an age when public speaking was an indispensable skill for every public man—even for a general in the field—and for every private man if he got involved in litigation. Rhetoric was then not so much the loveliest (*soavissima*) as the most practical of the arts. By the Middle Ages it has become literary. Its precepts are addressed quite as much to poets as to advocates. There is no antithesis, indeed no distinction, between Rhetoric and

Poetry. I think the Rhetoricians always have in view a pupil whose medium will be Latin, but their work also affected vernacular practice.

Chaucer's apostrophe to 'Gaufred, dere mayster souverain' in the *Nun's Priest's Tale* (B 4537) has kept alive the memory of Geoffrey de Vinsauf who 'flourished' about 1200 and wrote the *Nova Poetria*;[1] a work whose value lies in its extreme naivety.

He divides *Ordo* (which some call *Dispositio*) into two kinds, Natural and Artificial.[2] The Natural follows the King of Hearts' advice by beginning at the beginning. The Artificial is of three kinds. You can begin at the end (as in the *Oedipus Rex* or a play by Ibsen); or in the middle (like Virgil and Spenser); or with a *Sententia* or *Exemplum*. Chaucer begins with a *Sententia* or maxim in the *Parlement*, the *Hous of Fame*, the *Prologue to the Legend*, the *Legend of Phillis*, and the *Prioress's Tale*. I cannot remember that he ever begins with an *Exemplum*, but no one needs to be reminded how frequent they are in his work. The *Franklin's Tale* is held up from line 1367 to line 1456 by a procession of them, and Troilus had good reason to say to Pandarus

> What knowe I of the Quene Niobee?
> Lat be thyne olde ensaumples I thee preye.
>
> (I, 759.)

Here Geoffrey is dealing with a real problem, which we have all faced though few of us would pose it so bluntly. The Natural Order will not always serve. And

[1] Ed. Faral, *Les Arts Poétiques du XIIe et du XIIIe Siècles*.
[2] II, 100 *sq.*

the plan of beginning with a *Sententia*, or with something like it, is still an unlaid ghost. It 'walks' in that fatal opening paragraph with which schoolboys are apparently taught to begin their essays.

On *Amplificatio*[1] he is almost embarrassing. He calls the various methods of 'amplifying' your piece, quite frankly, *morae* (delays); as if the art of literature consisted in learning how to say much when you have little to say. That, I suspect, was how he really regarded it. But this means not that the *morae* he recommends are all necessarily bad but that he misunderstands—I do not profess to understand it fully myself—their real function.

One kind of *mora* is *Expolitio*. Its formula is 'Let the same thing be disguised by variety of form; be different yet the same'—

> multiplice forma
> Dissimuletur idem; varius sis et tamen idem.

It sounds dreadful. But it is not so in the Psalms, nor in

> Cut is the branch that might have grown full straight
> And burned is Apollo's laurel bough.

Less successful is

> When clouds are seen wise men put on their cloaks;
> When great leaves fall then winter is at hand;
> When the sun sets who does not look for night?
> Untimely storms make men expect a dearth.
>
> (*Richard III*, II, iii, 32 *sq.*)

Another is *Circumlocutio*. 'In order to lengthen the work don't call things by their names' (*Longius ut sit opus ne ponas nomina rerum*). Thus Dante calls dawn 'Old

[1] III, A 220 *sq.*

Tithonus' bedfellow', *la concubina di Titone antico*, in the *Purgatorio* (IX, I), or Chaucer at the opening of *Troilus*, III, instead of 'O Venus' writes

> O blisful light of which the bemes clere
> Adorneth at the thridde hevene faire,
> O sonnes lief, O Joves daughter dere,
> Pleasaunce of love, O goodly debonaire....

But the most important of all the *morae* is *Diversio* or Digression. Nearly all of us, when we first began reading medieval poetry, got the impression that the poets were unable to keep to the point. We may even have thought that they were drifting with the stream of consciousness. The revived study of medieval *Rhetoric*—a welcome novelty in twentieth-century medievalism—puts an end to that idea. For good or ill the digressiveness of the medieval writers is the product not of nature but of art. The second part of the *Romance of the Rose* depends on Digressions in the same degree, if not in the same way, as *Tristram Shandy*. It has even been suggested[1] that the peculiar narrative technique of the romances and of their Renaissance successors, the interwoven stories that so incessantly cross and interrupt one another, may be simply one more application of the digressive principle and an offshoot of Rhetoric.

This theory, which I do not myself fully accept, has at any rate the merit of replacing the Digressions recommended by Geoffrey in their proper context. They can be regarded as an expression of the same impulse we see at work in much medieval architecture and decoration. We

[1] See Vinaver, *Works of Malory*, vol. I, pp. xlviii *sq.*

may call it the love of the labyrinthine; the tendency to offer to the mind or the eye something that cannot be taken in at a glance, something that at first looks planless though all is planned. Everything leads to everything else, but by very intricate paths. At every point the question 'How did we get here?' arises, but there is always an answer. Professor Gunn[1] has done much towards enabling us to recover the taste by which such a structure could be enjoyed in literature; which could feel that the main subject, in throwing off so many digressions, which themselves throw off subordinate digressions, showed the ramifying energy of a strong tree, glorious with plenitude.

The other *morae* are *Apostropha* and *Descriptio*, which call for no comment.

On *Ornatus*, stylistic ornament, Geoffrey has a remarkable piece of advice: 'Do not always let a word remain in its natural position' (*noli semper concedere verbo In proprio residere loco*). What lies behind this is the practice of authors like Apuleius; in an inflected language such as Latin there is hardly any limit to the possible dislocations of idiomatic word-order. Yet Chaucer can go a long way in English, and so skilfully that we may not always be aware of it:

> The double sorwe of Troilus to tellen
> That was the King Priamus' sone of Troye,
> In loving how his aventures fellen
> Fro wo to wele and after out of ioye,
> My purpose is.... (*Troilus*, I, I *sq*).

[1] *The Mirror of Love* (Lubbock, Texas, 1952).

It goes down easily enough; but at no period of the English language would such a sentence have been possible in conversation. Nor was Chaucer the last poet to practise this nice derangement.

Two morals may possibly be drawn: (1) that the word-order in high medieval poetry can never, of itself, be evidence for that of the spoken language; and (2) that where a peculiarity of the order looks to us like a desperate concession to the demands of metre, this may not always be so.

How to end your composition, as well as how to begin it, was a problem. Matthew of Vendôme in his *Ars Versificatoria*[1] (late twelfth century) suggests five methods.[2]

One is *per epilogum*, that is *per recapitulationem sententiae*, by summing up the 'sentence' or moral of the whole. Chaucer thus ends the Tales of the Miller, the Reeve, and the Physician.

Another is by asking someone to amend your work; as Chaucer asks Gower at the end of *Troilus* (v, 1856).

The third is *per veniae petitionem*, by asking indulgence for your deficiencies. Gower uses this method in the *Confessio* (VIII, 3062, 1st version) and Hawes in the *Pastime of Pleasure* (5796).

The fourth is with a vaunt, *per ostensionem gloriae*. The classical precedent is Horace's *exegi monumentum*. Few, if any, medieval vernacular poets were bold enough to follow it.

Finally, you can end with the praise of God. Chaucer combines this with the second method in *Troilus* (v, 1863).

[1] See Faral, *op. cit.* [2] IV, xlix.

The Rhetorical precepts can be seen working at full blast in the *Phisicien's Tale*. Here is the analysis.

1–4	Story
5–29	*Descriptio* interrupted by *Prosopopoea* of Nature
30–71	*Descriptio* resumed
72–92	*Apostropha* to governesses
93–104	*Apostropha* to parents
105–239	Story
240–244	*Exemplum* of Jephthah's daughter
245–276	Story
277–286	Ending *per recapitulationem sententiae*

It works out at about ten lines of Amplification to every sixteen of narrative. The *Manciple's Tale* is equally rhetorical; in the *Pardoner's*, digression is used in a way that moderns find easier to enjoy.

The four Quadrivial Arts must here be summarily dismissed. Of Astronomy something has been said in an earlier chapter. On the vast and rewarding subject of medieval Music the reader must seek guides who are better qualified than I;[1] and Geometry, naturally, makes little impact on literature. It is, however, worth remembering that Arithmetic acquired during the Middle Ages an invaluable new tool—the so-called 'Arabic' numerals. The system is really of Indian origin and dates from the fifth century, but it reached the West through the work of the ninth-century mathematician Ben Musa, known as Al-Khowarazmi. A curious little eddy of errors and

[1] See *New Oxford History of Music*, vols. II and III; G. Reese, *Music in the Middle Ages* (New York, 1940) and *Music in the Renaissance* (New York, 1954); C. Parrish, *The Notation of Medieval Music* (1957); F. L. Harrison, *Music in Medieval Britain* (1958).

legends resulted. 'Al-Khowarazmi' (the man from Khawarazm) suggests an abstract noun *algorism*, later *augrim*, which means calculation. Hence 'figures of augrim' in the *Ancrene Wisse*. Then, to account for the word *algorism*, a mathematical sage Algus is invented, so that the *Roman de la Rose* speaks of

Algus, Euclidees, Tholomees.   (16,373.)

But in line 12,994 Algus had become Argus; in which form he slips into the *Book of the Duchess*—'Argus the noble countour'.

CHAPTER VIII

THE INFLUENCE OF THE MODEL

At sight of all this World beheld so faire.
MILTON

No one who has read the higher kinds of medieval and Renaissance poetry has failed to notice the amount of solid instruction—of science, philosophy, or history—that they carry. Sometimes, as in the *Divine Comedy* or Lyndsay's *Dreme* or Spenser's Mutability cantos, the theme is so chosen that it permits and invites such matter. Sometimes such matter is organically connected with a theme which, by our standards, seems well able to have dispensed with it; as the character and influence of the planets are worked into the *Knight's Tale* or the *Testament of Cresseid*. It may also seem to us to be 'dragged in by the heels' where, I believe, the medieval author would have felt it to be wholly relevant. When the poet of *Gawain* begins with the fall of Troy he is not merely padding. He is obeying the principle of 'a place for everything and everything in its right place'; fitting Gawain through Arthur and Arthur through Brut and Brut through Troy into the total 'historial' Model. The commonest method, however, is by digression; such digressions as we find in the *Roman de la Rose* on Fortune (4837–5070), on free will (17,101–778), on true nobility (18,589–896), on the function and limitations of Nature (15,891–16,974), on the merely derivative immortality of gods or angels (19,063–112). In places readers may

disagree as to how far a piece of cosmology or metaphysics constitutes a digression. The long dramat-
isation (in a Christianised form) of Aristotle's distinction
between Nature and the realm above her which occupies
Deguileville's *Pèlerinage* from line 3344 to line 3936 (of
Lydgate's version) may be thought relevant. And some
think that the treatment of free will in *Troilus*, v, is no
digression.

The simplest form in which this tendency expresses
itself is mere catalogue. We have in Bernardus catalogues
of Hierarchies, stars, mountains, beasts, rivers, woods,
vegetables, fish, and birds (I Metr. III); in the *Hous of
Fame*, of musicians (III, 1201 *sq.*); in the *Franklin's Tale*, of
virtuous women (F 1367 *sq.*); in the *King's Quair*, of
beasts (st. 155–7); in the *Temple of Glas*, of famous lovers
(55 *sq.*); in Henryson's *Trial of the Fox*, of beasts (*Fables*,
881 *sq.*); in the *Court of Sapience*, stones (953 *sq.*), fish
(1198 *sq.*), flowers (1282 *sq.*), trees (1374 *sq.*), birds and
beasts (1387 *sq.*). In Douglas' *Palice of Honour* we have
sages, lovers, Muses, mountains, rivers, and 'nobill men
and women both of scripture and gentyll stories'. The
whole plan of Petrarch's *Trionfi* seems to be devised for
the purpose of admitting as many catalogues as possible.

At first one suspects pedantry, but that can hardly be
the true explanation. Much, though not all, of the knowledge was too common to reflect any particular distinction on an author. Henryson might expect, and justly, to
be admired for describing the characters of the planets so
vividly; hardly for knowing them. The same objection
holds against the view which I took when, years ago, I

first dealt with medieval literature. I thought that in an age when books were few and the intellectual appetite sharp-set, any knowledge might be welcome in any context. But this does not explain why the authors so gladly present knowledge which most of their audience must have possessed. One gets the impression that ·medieval people, like Professor Tolkien's Hobbits, enjoyed books which told them what they already knew.

Another explanation might be based in Rhetoric. Rhetoric recommended *morae*—delays or padding. Does all this science and 'story' come in simply *longius ut sit opus*, 'that the work may be longer'? But this perhaps overlooks the fact that Rhetoric explains the formal, not the material, characteristic. That is, it may tell you to digress; not what to put into your digressions. It may approve Common Places; it can hardly decide what shall achieve the status of a Common Place. From reading Dr Curtius[1] on the *locus amoenus*, that pleasant woodland scene at which so many poets tried their hand, an unwary reader might get a wrong impression (which naturally I do not attribute to Dr Curtius himself). He might think that Rhetoric accounted not only for the treatment of this Common Place but for the popularity that made it common. But Rhetoric is no such closed system. It is Nature—the character of shifting light and shade, of trees and running water and a gentle breeze, and their effect on human nerves and emotions—which caused the *locus* to be *amoenus*, and only therefore to be *communis*. In the same way, if all the catalogues and digressions are filled with a

[1] *European Literature and the Latin Middle Ages*, pp. 195 *sq.*

certain sort of matter, this must be because writers and their audience liked it. Digression need not deal with the large, permanent features of the universe unless you want. The long-tailed similes in Homer or the 'episodes' in Thomson usually do not. They are more often 'vignettes'.

Again, the Rhetorical explanation could hardly be extended to cover the visible arts, where we are met with the same phenomenon. They also continually re-state what was believed about the universe. I have already mentioned[1] the cupola above Chigi's tomb which magnificently re-states the Boethian doctrine of Providence and Destiny. It does not stand alone. The planets look down from the capitals in the Doge's palace, each surrounded by his 'children', by the mortals who exhibit his influence.[2] At Florence they meet us again, strangely disguised by the influence of Saracenic iconography, in Santa Maria del Fiore;[3] and again in Santa Maria Novella, paired off, after the manner of the *Convivio*, with the Seven Liberal Arts.[4] The Salone (Palazzo della Ragione) at Padua[5] is, in a different art, a close parallel to Spenser's Mutability cantos. We have the planets, their children, the Zodiacal signs, the Apostles, and the labours of men all arranged under their appropriate months.

And just as the planets are not merely present in the *Testament of Cresseid* but woven into the plot, so in the buildings the cosmological material is sometimes woven into what we may call the plot of a building. One might at first suppose that the constellations depicted on the

[1] See above, p. 87. [2] Seznec, *op. cit.* fig. 21.
[3] *Ibid.* fig. 63. [4] *Ibid.* fig. 22. [5] *Ibid.* p. 73.

cupola above the altar in the old sacristy of San Lorenzo
at Florence were mere decoration; but they are in the
right positions for 9 July 1422 when the altar was con-
secrated.[1] In the Farnesina Palace they are arranged to
suit the birth-day of Chigi for whom the work was done.[2]
And the Salone at Padua is apparently designed so that at
each sunrise the beams will fall on the Sign in which Sol
would then ride.

The lost art of Pageant loved to re-state similar themes.
And it has lately been shown that many Renaissance pictures which were once thought purely fanciful are
loaded, and almost overloaded, with philosophy.[3]

Here, as at the outset of this book, we see a striking yet
deceptive parallel between medieval and savage behaviour.
This labour to reproduce in earthly mimicry the great
operations of nature[4] looks very like the savage's attempt
to control or encourage such operations by imitating
them—to bring rain by making a noise as like a thunder-
storm as a man with a stick and a tom-tom can achieve.
But medieval and Renaissance credulity ran in the
opposite direction. Men were far less prone to think they
could control the translunary forces than to think that
those forces controlled them. Astrological determinism,
not imitative magic, was the real danger.

The simplest explanation is, I believe, the true one.
Poets and other artists depicted these things because their

[1] Seznec, *op. cit.* p. 77. [2] *Ibid.* p. 79.

[3] See E. Wind, *Pagan Mysteries in the Renaissance* (1958).

[4] 'Most of the first clocks were less chronometers than exhibitions of
the pattern of the universe' (L. White, Jr., *Medieval Technology and
Social Change*, Oxford, 1962, p. 122).

minds loved to dwell on them. Other ages have not had a Model so universally accepted as theirs, so imaginable, and so satisfying to the imagination. Marcus Aurelius[1] wished that men would love the universe as a man can love his own city. I believe that something like this was really possible in the period I am discussing. At least, fairly like it. The medieval and Renaissance delight in the universe was, I think, more spontaneous and aesthetic, less laden with conscience and resignation, than anything the Stoical emperor had in mind. It was, though not in any Wordsworthian sense, a 'love of nature'.

Merely to imitate or to comment on the human life around us was therefore not felt to be the sole function of the arts. The labours of men appear on Achilles''shield in Homer for their own sake. In the Mutability cantos or the Salone they appear not only for their own sake but also because of their relation to the months, and therefore to the Zodiac, and therefore to the whole natural order. This does not at all mean that where Homer was disinterested the later artist was didactic. It means that where Homer rejoiced in the particulars the later artist rejoiced also in that great imagined structure which gave them all their place. Every particular fact and story became more interesting and more pleasurable if, by being properly fitted in, it carried one's mind back to the Model as a whole.

If I am right, the man of genius then found himself in a situation very different from that of his modern successor. Such a man today often, perhaps usually, feels himself

[1] IV, 23.

confronted with a reality whose significance he cannot know, or a reality that has no significance; or even a reality such that the very question whether it has a meaning is itself a meaningless question. It is for him, by his own sensibility, to discover a meaning, or, out of his own subjectivity, to give a meaning—or at least a shape—to what in itself had neither. But the Model universe of our ancestors had a built-in significance. And that in two senses; as having 'significant form' (it is an admirable design) and as a manifestation of the wisdom and goodness that created it. There was no question of waking it into beauty or life. Ours, most emphatically, was not the wedding garment, nor the shroud. The achieved perfection was already there. The only difficulty was to make an adequate response.

This, if accepted, will perhaps go far to explain some characteristics of medieval literature.

It may, for example, explain both its most typical vice and its most typical virtue. The typical vice, as we all know, is dulness; sheer, unabashed, prolonged dulness, where the author does not seem to be even trying to interest us. The *South English Legendary* or *Ormulum* or parts of Hoccleve are good examples. One sees how the belief in a world of built-in significance encourages this. The writer feels everything to be so interesting in itself that there is no need for him to make it so. The story, however badly told, will still be worth telling; the truths, however badly stated, still worth stating. He expects the subject to do for him nearly everything he ought to do himself. Outside literature we can still see this state of mind at work. On the lowest intellectual level, people who find any one subject entirely engrossing are apt to think that any reference to it, of whatever quality, must have some value. Pious people on that level appear to think that the quotation of any scriptural text, or any line from a hymn, or even any noise made by a harmonium, is an edifying sermon or a cogent apologetic. Less pious people on the same level, dull clowns, seem to think that they have achieved either a voluptuous or a comic effect—I am not sure which is intended—by chalking up a single indecent word on a wall. The presence of a Model whose significance is 'given' is likewise no unmixed blessing.

And yet, I believe, it is also connected with the characteristic virtue of good medieval work. What this is, anyone can feel if he turns from the narrative verse of, say, Chapman or Keats to the best parts of Marie de France or Gower. What will strike him at once is the absence of strain. In the Elizabethan or Romantic examples we feel that the poet has done a great deal of work; in the medieval, we are at first hardly aware of a poet at all. The writing is so limpid and effortless that the story seems to be telling itself. You would think, till you tried, that anyone could do the like. But in reality no story tells itself. Art is at work. But it is the art of people who, no less than the bad medieval authors, have a complete confidence in the intrinsic value of their matter. The telling is for the sake of the tale; in Chapman or Keats we feel that the tale is valued only as an opportunity for the lavish and highly individual treatment. We feel the same difference on turning from Sidney's *Arcadia* to Malory's *Morte*, or from a battle in Drayton to one in Laȝamon. I am not suggesting a preference, for both ways of writing can be good; I am only underlining a difference.

With this attitude goes the characteristically medieval type of imagination.[1] It is not a transforming imagination like Wordsworth's or a penetrative imagination like Shakespeare's. It is a realising imagination. Macaulay noted in Dante the extremely factual word-painting; the details, the comparisons, designed at whatever cost of dignity to make sure that we see exactly what he saw. Now Dante in this is typically medieval. The Middle Ages are unrivalled, till we reach quite modern times, in the sheer foreground fact, the 'close-up'. I mean things like the little dog's behaviour in the *Book of the Duchess*; or 'So stant Custance and looketh hire aboute'; or, of Constance again, 'ever she prayeth hire child to hold his pees'; or, when Arcite and Palamon met for the combat, 'Tho chaungen gan the colour in hir face'; or the reluctance of the ladies-in-waiting to handle Griselda's clothes. But not by any means only in Chaucer. I mean the young Arthur turning alternately pale and red in Laȝamon, or Merlin twisting like a snake in his prophetic trance; and Jonah in *Patience* going into the whale's mouth 'like a mote at a minster door'; and in Malory all the practical and financial detail and even Guenever's recognisable cough; or the fairy bakers rubbing the paste off their fingers in *Huon*; or Henryson's ineffective mouse running

---

[1] See also E. Auerbach, *Mimesis* (Berne, 1946), trans. W. Trask, Princeton, 1957.

up and down the river bank with many a 'pitous peep'. We even see the Almighty 'laughing His heart sore' at the old alewife in *Kynd Kittok*. This sort of vividness is now part of every novelist's stock-in-trade; a tool of our rhetoric, often used to excess so that it hides rather than reveals the action. But the medievals had hardly any models for it, and it was long before they had many successors.[1]

Two negative conditions made it possible: their freedom both from the pseudo-classical standard of decorum and from the sense of period. But the efficient cause

[1] At first the reader may complain that the quality I am describing is simply the character of all good imaginative writing whatever. I believe not. In Racine there are no foreground facts at all, nothing for our senses. Virgil relies chiefly on atmosphere, sound, and association. In *Paradise Lost* (as its theme demands) the art lies less in making us imagine the concrete than in making us believe we have imagined the unimaginable. Homer, had they known him, could have helped the medievals. Two details—the baby's fear of the plumed helmet and Andromache's tearful smile (*Iliad*, VI, 466–84)—are very much in their manner. But in general his art is not very like theirs. The detailed descriptions of work—launching a ship, preparing a meal—by being formalised and constantly repeated produce a quite different effect. We feel not the seized moment but the changeless pattern of life. He brings his people before us almost entirely by making them talk. Even so, their language is distanced by the epic formula; song, not speech. Eurycleia, the moment she has recognised her old master, promises him a confidential report on the behaviour of the domestics during his absence (*Odyssey*, XIX, 495–8). The Old Family Servant is pin-pointed forever. We read her mind, but we do not actually hear her voice. Not as we hear Launcelot's fumbling reiteration 'And therefore, madam, I was but late in that quest' (Malory, XVIII, 2), or Chaucer's monosyllabic replies to the eagle (*Hous of Fame*, III, 864, 888, 913). Indeed it may be doubted whether the characteristic merits of the four great poets I have mentioned (Racine, Virgil, Milton, Homer) are even compatible with the medieval vividness. No one kind of work admits every excellence.

surely was their devout attention to their matter and their confidence in it. They are not trying to heighten it or transform it. It possesses them wholly. Their eyes and ears are steadily fixed upon it, and so—perhaps hardly aware how much they are inventing—they see and hear what the event must have been like.

Admittedly, there is in some of their writing much ornament and even, as may be thought, affectation; especially when they use Latin. But it is, and not in a necessarily pejorative sense, superficial. The author's basic attitude remains free from strain or posturing. He rubricates and aureates to honour a theme which for him, and by common consent, ought to be honoured. He is not at all doing the sort of thing that Donne did when he built a poem (and a good one) out of the thesis—in cold prose it is mere raving—that the death of Elizabeth Drury was a more or less cosmic catastrophe. A medieval poet, wrongly but not unintelligibly, would have thought that silly. When Dunbar heavily gilds his verse it is to celebrate the Nativity or, at least, a royal marriage. He wears ceremonial robes because he is taking part in a ceremony. He is not 'stunting'.

When we meet bad poetry in different traditions, poetry that claims more for itself and its poet, we may say that we can 'see *through* it'. The rubble can be detected through the stucco. But the glory of the best medieval work often consists precisely in the fact that we *see* through it; it is a pure transparency.

One curious characteristic remains to be noticed. Many of the vivid close-ups are original additions to works which are not, as a whole, original. It is astonishing how often this occurs. One is tempted to say that almost the typical activity of the medieval author consists in touching up something that was already there; as Chaucer touched up Boccaccio, as Malory touched up French prose romances which themselves touched up earlier romances in verse, as Laȝamon works over Wace, who works over Geoffrey, who works over no one knows what. We are inclined to wonder how men could be at once so original that they handled no predecessor without pouring new life into him, and so unoriginal that they seldom did anything completely new. The predecessor is usually much more than a 'source' in the sense in which an Italian novel may be the source of a Shakespearian play. Shakespeare takes a few bones from the novel's plot and flings the rest to well-deserved oblivion. Round those bones he builds a new work whose purport, atmosphere, and language have really nothing in common with his original. Chaucer's *Troilus* stands in a very different relation to the *Filostrato*.

If an artist made alterations in someone else's picture which covered about a third of the canvas, we should deceive ourselves in trying by mere measurements to assess the contribution of each painter to the total effect. For the work done by every mass and colour in the new patches will be affected through and through by the parts of the original which still remain; and in them every mass and colour will similarly be affected by the new patches. We should have to think of the total result chemically rather than arithmetically. It is like that when Chaucer works over Boccaccio. No line, however closely translated, will do exactly what it did in the Italian once Chaucer has made his additions. No line in those additions but depends for much of its effect on the translated lines which precede and follow it. The poem as we now have it cannot be attributed to a single author. Still less can the work we call Malory's.

It follows that the book–author unit, basic for modern criticism, must often be abandoned when we are dealing with medieval literature. Some books—if I may use a comparison I have used elsewhere—must be regarded more as we regard those cathedrals where work of many different periods is mixed and produces a total effect, admirable indeed but never foreseen nor intended by any one of the successive builders. Many generations, each in its own spirit and its own style, have contributed to the story of Arthur. It is misleading to think of Malory as an author in our modern sense and throw all the earlier work into the category of 'sources'. He is merely the last builder, doing a few demolitions here and adding a few features there. They cannot make the work his as *Vanity Fair* is Thackeray's.

It would have been impossible for men to work in this way if they had had anything like our conception of literary property. But it would also have been impossible unless their idea of literature had differed from ours on a deeper level. Far from feigning originality, as a modern plagiarist would, they are apt to conceal it. They sometimes profess to be deriving something from their *auctour* at the very moment when they are departing from him.

It cannot be a joke. What is funny about it? And who but a scholar could see the point if it were? They are behaving more like a historian who misrepresents the documents because he feels sure that things must have happened in a certain way. They are anxious to convince others, perhaps to half-convince themselves, that they are not merely 'making things up'. For the aim is not self-expression or 'creation'; it is to hand on the 'historial' matter worthily; not worthily of your own genius or of the poetic art but of the matter itself.

I doubt if they would have understood our demand for originality or valued those works in their own age which were original any the more on that account. If you had asked Laȝamon or Chaucer 'Why do you not make up a brand-new story of your own?' I think they might have replied (in effect) 'Surely we are not yet reduced to that?' Spin something out of one's own head when the world teems with so many noble deeds, wholesome examples, pitiful tragedies, strange adventures, and merry jests which have never yet been set forth quite so well as they deserve? The originality which we regard as a sign of wealth might have seemed to them a confession of poverty. Why make things for oneself like the lonely Robinson Crusoe when there is riches all about you to be had for the taking? The modern artist often does not think the riches is there. He is the alchemist who must turn base metal into gold. It makes a radical difference.

And the paradox is that it is just this abdication of originality which brings out the originality they really possess. The more devout and concentrated Chaucer's gaze on the *Filostrato* becomes, or Malory's on the 'French Book', the more real the scenes and people become to them. That reality forces them presently to see and hear, hence to set down, at first a little more, and then a good deal more, than their book has actually told them. They are thus never more indebted to their *auctour* than when they are adding to him. If they had been less rapt by what they read they would have reproduced him more faithfully. We should think it 'cheek', an unpardonable liberty, half to translate and half to re-write another man's work. But Chaucer and Malory were not thinking of their *auctour*'s claims. They were thinking—the *auctour*'s success lay in making them think—about Troilus or Launcelot.

As we have already seen,[1] the very awareness that their *auctour* wrote fiction and that their additions to him were further fiction seems to have been dim and wavering. Historians, from Herodotus to Milton, handed the responsibility for truth over to their sources; conversely, writers of Troy Books talk as if they were historians who had weighed their authorities. Even Chaucer does not praise Homer for his 'feyninge' but blames him for lying, like the Greek partisan he was (*Hous of Fame*, III, 1477–9), and puts him in the same class with Josephus (1430–81). I do not suppose that Chaucer and, say, Laȝamon both had exactly the same attitude to their material. But I doubt if either, like the modern novelist, felt that he was 'creative' or thought that his source had

[1] See above, pp. 178–82.

been so. And I think the majority[1] of the audience, then as now, could hardly conceive the activity of invention at all. It is said that people pointed out Dante in the street not as the man who made the *Comedy* but as the man who had been in Hell. Even today there are those (some of them critics) who believe every novel and even every lyric to be autobiographical. A man who lacks invention himself does not easily attribute it to others. Perhaps in the Middle Ages those who had it did not easily attribute it to themselves.

The most surprising thing in the *Hous of Fame* is that the poets (with one historian) are present not because they are famous but to support the fame of their subjects. Josephus in that House 'bar upon his shuldres hye' the fame of Jewry (III, 1435–6); Homer, with many such colleagues as Dares and Guido, that of Troy (1455–80); Virgil, that of Aeneas (1485). The medievals were, indeed, fully conscious (Dante especially)[2] that poets not only gave but also won fame. But in the last resort it is the fame they give—the fame of Aeneas, not of Virgil—that really matters. That Edward King should now be remembered at all only because he gave occasion to *Lycidas* would perhaps have seemed to them a strange inversion. If Milton had been by their standards a successful poet he would now be remembered for 'bearing up' the fame of Edward King.

---

[1] A notable exception is the King who thought *lygisogur skemtilagastar* (lying sagas the most entertaining) (see *Sturlunga Saga*, ed. O. Brown, 1952, p. 19).

[2] *De Vulg. Eloquentia*, I, xvii; *Purgatorio*, XXI, 85.

When Pope re-wrote the *Hous of Fame* as his *Temple of Fame* he quietly altered this passage. The poets are in his Temple because they have won fame. Between Chaucer's time and his the arts had become conscious of what is now regarded as their true status. Since his time they have become even more so. One almost foresees the day when they may be conscious of little else.

Hence we may, with proper precautions, regard a certain humility as the overall characteristic of medieval art. Of the art; not always of the artists. Self-esteem may arise within any occupation at any period. A chef, a surgeon, or a scholar, may be proud, even to arrogance, of his skill; but his skill is confessedly the means to an end beyond itself, and the status of the skill depends wholly on the dignity or necessity of that end. I think it was then like that with all the arts. Literature exists to teach what is useful, to honour what deserves honour, to appreciate what is delightful. The useful, honourable, and delightful things are superior to it: it exists for their sake; its own use, honour, or delightfulness is derivative from theirs. In that sense the art is humble even when the artists are proud; proud of their proficiency in the art, but not making for the art itself the high Renaissance or Romantic claims. Perhaps they might not all have fully agreed with the statement that poetry is *infima inter omnes doctrinas*.[1] But it awoke no such hurricane of protest as it would awake today.

In this great change something has been won and something lost. I take it to be part and parcel of the same

[1] Aquinas Iª, 1, Art. 9.

great process of Internalisation[1] which has turned *genius* from an attendant *daemon* into a quality of the mind. Always, century by century, item after item is transferred from the object's side of the account to the subject's. And now, in some extreme forms of Behaviourism, the subject himself is discounted as merely subjective; we only think that we think. Having eaten up everything else, he eats himself up too. And where we 'go from that' is a dark question.

[1] See above, p. 42.

EPILOGUE

The best in this kind are but shadows.
SHAKESPEARE

I have made no serious effort to hide the fact that the old Model delights me as I believe it delighted our ancestors. Few constructions of the imagination seem to me to have combined splendour, sobriety, and coherence in the same degree. It is possible that some readers have long been itching to remind me that it had a serious defect; it was not true.

I agree. It was not true. But I would like to end by saying that this charge can no longer have exactly the same sort of weight for us that it would have had in the nineteenth century. We then claimed, as we still claim, to know much more about the real universe than the medievals did; and hoped, as we still hope, to discover yet more truths about it in the future. But the meaning of the words 'know' and 'truth' in this context has begun to undergo a certain change.

The nineteenth century still held the belief that by inferences from our sense-experience (improved by instruments) we could 'know' the ultimate physical reality more or less as, by maps, pictures, and travel-books, a man can 'know' a country he has not visited; and that in both cases the 'truth' would be a sort of mental replica of the thing itself. Philosophers might have disquieting comments to make on this conception; but scientists and plain men did not much attend to them.

Already, to be sure, mathematics were the idiom in

which many of the sciences spoke. But I do not think it was doubted that there was a concrete reality *about* which the mathematics held good; distinguishable from the mathematics as a heap of apples is from the process of counting them. We knew indeed that it was in some respects not adequately imaginable; quantities and distances if either very small or very great could not be visualised. But, apart from that, we hoped that ordinary imagination and conception could grasp it. We should then have through mathematics a knowledge not merely mathematical. We should be like the man coming to know about a foreign country without visiting it. He learns about the mountains from carefully studying the contour lines on a map. But his knowledge is not a knowledge *of* contour lines. The real knowledge is achieved when these enable him to say 'That would be an easy ascent', 'This is a dangerous precipice', 'A would not be visible from B', 'These woods and waters must make a pleasant valley'. In going beyond the contour lines to such conclusions he is (if he knows how to read a map) getting nearer to the reality.

It would be very different if someone said to him (and was believed) 'But it is the contour lines themselves that are the fullest reality you can get. In turning away from them to these other statements you are getting further from the reality, not nearer. All those ideas about "real" rocks and slopes and views are merely a metaphor or a parable; a *pis aller*, permissible as a concession to the weakness of those who can't understand contour lines, but misleading if they are taken literally.'

And this, if I understand the situation, is just what has now happened as regards the physical sciences. The mathematics are now the nearest to the reality we can get. Anything imaginable, even anything that can be manipulated by ordinary (that is, non-mathematical) conceptions, far from being a further truth to which mathematics were the avenue, is a mere analogy, a concession to our weakness. Without a parable modern physics speaks not to the multitudes. Even among themselves, when they attempt to verbalise their findings, the scientists begin to speak of this as making 'models'. It is from them that I have borrowed the word. But these 'models' are not, like model ships, small-scale replicas of the reality. Sometimes they illustrate this or that aspect of it by an analogy. Sometimes, they do not illustrate but merely suggest, like the sayings of the mystics. An expression such as 'the curvature of space' is strictly comparable to the old definition of God as 'a circle whose centre is everywhere and whose circumference is nowhere'. Both succeed in suggesting; each does so by offering what is, on the level of our ordinary thinking, nonsense. By accepting the 'curvature of space' we are not 'knowing' or enjoying 'truth' in the fashion that was once thought to be possible.

It would therefore be subtly misleading to say 'The medievals thought the universe to be like that, but we know it to be like this'. Part of what we now know is that we cannot, in the old sense, 'know what the universe is like' and that no model we can build will be, in that old sense, 'like' it.

Epilogue

Again, such a statement would suggest that the old Model gave way simply under the pressure of newly discovered phenomena—as a detective's original theory of the crime might yield to the discovery that his first suspect had an unassailable *alibi*. And this certainly happened as regards many particular details in the old Model, just as it happens daily to particular hypotheses in a modern laboratory. Exploration refuted the belief that the tropics are too hot for life; the first *nova* refuted the belief that the translunary realm is immutable. But the change of the Model as a whole was not so simple an affair.

The most spectacular differences between the Medieval Model and our own concern astronomy and biology. In both fields the new Model is supported by a wealth of empirical evidence. But we should misrepresent the historical process if we said that the irruption of new facts was the sole cause of the alteration.

The old astronomy was not, in any exact sense, 'refuted' by the telescope. The scarred surface of the Moon and the satellites of Jupiter can, if one wants, be fitted into a geocentric scheme. Even the enormous, and enormously different, distances of the stars can be accommodated if you are prepared to make their 'sphere', the *stellatum*, of a vast thickness. The old scheme, 'with Centric and Eccentric scribl'd o're', had been tinkered a good deal to keep up with observations. How far, by endless tinkerings, it could have kept up with them till even now, I do not know. But the human mind will not long endure such ever-increasing complications if once it has seen that some simpler conception can 'save the appearances'. Neither theological prejudice nor vested interests can permanently keep in favour a Model which is seen to be grossly uneconomical. The new astronomy triumphed not because the case for the old became desperate, but because the new was a better tool; once this was grasped, our ingrained conviction that Nature herself is thrifty did the rest. When our Model is in its turn abandoned, this conviction will no doubt be at work again. What models we should build, or whether we could build any, if some great alteration in human psychology withdrew this conviction, is an interesting question.

But the change of Models did not involve astronomy alone. It involved also, in biology, the change—arguably more important—from a devolutionary to an evolutionary scheme; from a cosmology in which it was axiomatic that 'all perfect things precede all imperfect things'[1] to one in which it is axiomatic that 'the starting point (*Entwicklungsgrund*) is always lower than what is developed' (the degree of change can be gauged by the fact that *primitive* is now in most contexts a pejorative term).

This revolution was certainly not brought about by the discovery of new facts. When I was a boy I believed that 'Darwin discovered evolution' and that the far more general, radical, and even cosmic developmentalism which till lately dominated all popular thought was a superstructure raised on the biological theorem. This view has been sufficiently disproved.[2] The statement which I have just quoted about the *Entwicklungsgrund* was made by

[1] See above, p. 85.   [2] See Lovejoy, *op. cit.* cap. ix.

Epilogue

Schelling in 1812. In him, in Keats, in Wagner's tetralogy, in Goethe, in Herder, the change to the new point of view has already taken place. Its growth can be traced far further back in Leibniz, Akenside, Kant, Maupertuis, Diderot. Already in 1786 Robinet believes in an 'active principle' which overcomes brute matter, and *la progression n'est pas finie*. For him, as for Bergson or de Chardin, the 'gates of the future are wide open'. The demand for a developing world—a demand obviously in harmony both with the revolutionary and the romantic temper—grows up first; when it is full grown the scientists go to work and discover the evidence on which our belief in that sort of universe would now be held to rest. There is no question here of the old Model's being shattered by the inrush of new phenomena. The truth would seem to be the reverse; that when changes in the human mind produce a sufficient disrelish of the old Model and a sufficient hankering for some new one, phenomena to support that new one will obediently turn up. I do not at all mean that these new phenomena are illusory. Nature has all sorts of phenomena in stock and can suit many different tastes.

An interesting astronomical change in our Model is going on at present. Fifty years ago, if you asked an astronomer about 'life on other worlds', he was apt to be totally agnostic about it or even to stress its improbability. We are now told that in so vast a universe stars that have planets and planets that have inhabitants must occur times without number. Yet no compulsive evidence is to hand. But is it irrelevant that in between the old opinion and the new we have had the vast proliferation of 'science fiction' and the beginnings of space-travel in real life?

I hope no one will think that I am recommending a return to the Medieval Model. I am only suggesting considerations that may induce us to regard all Models in the right way, respecting each and idolising none. We are all, very properly, familiar with the idea that in every age the human mind is deeply influenced by the accepted Model of the universe. But there is a two-way traffic; the Model is also influenced by the prevailing temper of mind. We must recognise that what has been called 'a taste in universes' is not only pardonable but inevitable. We can no longer dismiss the change of Models as a simple progress from error to truth. No Model is a catalogue of ultimate realities, and none is a mere fantasy. Each is a serious attempt to get in all the phenomena known at a given period, and each succeeds in getting in a great many. But also, no less surely, each reflects the prevalent psychology of an age almost as much as it reflects the state of that age's knowledge. Hardly any battery of new facts could have persuaded a Greek that the universe had an attribute so repugnant to him as infinity; hardly any such battery could persuade a modern that it is hierarchical.

It is not impossible that our own Model will die a violent death, ruthlessly smashed by an unprovoked assault of new facts—unprovoked as the *nova* of 1572. But I think it is more likely to change when, and because, far-reaching changes in the mental temper of our descendants demand that it should. The new Model will not be set up without evidence, but the evidence will turn up when the inner need for it becomes sufficiently great. It will be true evidence. But nature gives most of her evidence in answer to the questions we ask her. Here, as in the courts, the character of the evidence depends on the shape of the examination, and a good cross-examiner can do wonders. He will not indeed elicit falsehoods from an honest witness. But, in relation to the total truth in the witness's mind, the structure of the examination is like a stencil. It determines how much of that total truth will appear and what pattern it will suggest.

INDEX

Abercrombie, L., 133 n.

Abora, 145

Abyssinia, 144–5

Adam, 156, 183

Aelian, 147

Aesopic fable, 65, 147

Aether, why posited, 4; its frontier with air, 32–3; its animals, 41; Fifth Element or Quintessence, 95; in nineteenth century, 167

Air, extends to Moon, 4, 108, 117; frontier with aether, 33; its animals, 41; mediates influences, 110

Akenside, 221

Alanus ab Insulis, *De Planctu Naturae*, 35–6; suburbanises man, 58; *Anticlaudianus*, 60; on fame, 81; degrades daemons to demons, 118; mentioned, 80, 153, 166, 167

Albertus Magnus, on planetary images, 104; on the relation of an Intelligence to his sphere, 115–16; on the Wits, 162–4; mentioned, 18, 31

Albinus, 60

Alexander, 144, 181

Alfred, 75, 84, 181

Algus, 197

Al-Khowarazmi, 196–7

Almagest, 22, 22 n.

Amara, 145

Ambrose, St, 150

Amyclas, *v.* Lucan

Ancrene Wisse, 197

angels, or gods, 40–2; aetherial creatures, 56, 109; pictures of, merely symbolical, 71; species of, etc., 71–4; demoted, 135–6

Anima in neo-Platonic Trinity, 67

animals, aetherial and aerial, 41, 115; terrestrial, 146–52

Annunciation, the, why made by an angel, 73

anthropoperipheral universe, 51, 55, 57–8, 63, 116

antipodes, *v.* earth

Apuleius, on daemons, 2, 40–2; the Triad and Plenitude, 43–4; influence on style, 194; mentioned, 72, 117, 166

Aquinas, Thomas, on hypotheses, 16; the Annunciation, 73; planetary influences, 103; relation of an Intelligence to his sphere, 115–16; all daemons are demons, 118; Last Fire will not destroy translunary world, 121 n.; human soul, 154–5; status of poetry, 214; mentioned, 10, 12, 19

Areopagus, 70

Argus, *v.* Algus

Ariosto, 8, 176

Aristotle, on imperfect regularity of nature, 3; Nature and Sky, 3–4, 32, 37; censured by Chalcidius, 59; on στέρησις of Form in matter, 59; the Supercelestial, 96–7; the Prime Mover, 113, 114; on 'right reason', 160; his Ode to Virtue, 161; mentioned, 10, 19, 199

Arithmetic, 186, 196–7

Arnold, Matthew, 10, 80

Artemidorus, 63

Arthur, 179, 181, 182, 183

Arts, the Seven Liberal, 185–97, 201

Ashe, G., 146 n.

astrology, 103–9

Auerbach, E., 206 n.

augrim, 197

Augustine, St, on the *Platonici*, 49; the Last Fire, 121 n.; Adam's pre-existence, 155–6; mentioned, 50, 107 n., 168, 175

224

Index

Index

Index

Elfame, Queen of, 124
Elizabeth I, 75, 124
Elyot, Thomas, on the Complexions, 171-3
Empedocles, 50, 56
end of the world, ends only the sublunary realm, 120-1
Epicureans, 85
Er (in Plato), 23, 65
Erictho, 32, 39
eternity, 89, 114
eumenis, a trans. for *elf*, 124
Exeter Book, the, 150
Existenialists, 81

fairies, the three conceptions, 123-4; terrible fairies, 124-6; miniature fairies, 127-30; High Fairies, 130-4; attempts to fit them in, 134-8
Faral, 191 n.
Farnesina Palace, 202
fate (pl.), *v.* fairies
feel, to prove empirically, 189-90
Ficino, 156
Fielding, 83, 159
filii mortuae, 136
Fire, element of, 95-6
Florence, 201, 202
Fortuna Major, 106
Fortuna Minor, 107
Fortune, in Boethius, 81-2; in Dante, 82, 139-40; concept of hostile to historicism, 176-7
French tragedy, 81, 207 n.
Freud, 14, 54
Froissart, 177, 178, 182

Galileo, 16
Gallio, 29
Gawain and the Green Knight, 126, 130, 147, 198
Genesis, 51
genius, 42, 215
Geoffrey of Monmouth, 2, 209
Geoffrey de Vinsauf, 191-5

Geste Hystoriale of Troy, 178
Gibbon, 90, 183
Giraldus, Cambrensis, 126
glamour, 187
Gnomes, 135
Gobi desert, 145-6
Godfrey of Bouillon, 181
Goethe, 221
Gombrich, E. H., 101 n.
Gower, on fame, 81; nobility, 85; *kindly enclyning*, 92; grades of being, 93 n., 153 n.; Mercury, 107; the Sublunary, 108; Luna, 109; *faierie*, 124, 130-1, 136; world's end, 143; decadence, 184; Carmente, 187 n.; mentioned, 105, 195, 205
Grammar, 186-8
Grammary, 187
Granusion, 59-60
Gregory, 93 n., 153
Guido delle Colonne, 213
Guillaume de Lorris, 161
Gulliver, 102, 127
gumphi, 60, 167
Gunn, A. M. F., 194

Haldane, J. B. S., 97 n.
Harrison, F. L. S., 196 n.
Hawes, 195
Hecataeus, 62
Hector, 181, 183, 185
Hegel, 175, 176, 189
heimskringla, the world, 141
Heliodorus, 31
Henryson, on music of the spheres, 112; catalogue in, 199; on planets, 198, 201; mentioned, 206
Herder, 221
Herodotus, his conception of the historian's duty, 179-80; mentioned, 62, 147, 212
Hesiod, 50, 65, 66
Heylin, Peter, 145
High Fairies, 130-4
Hipparchus, 4 n.
historicism, 82, 174-7

227

Index

Hoccleve, 204

Holinshed, 125

Homer, ultimate source of Isidore's weeping horses?, 148; his shield contrasted with Spenser and the Salone, 203; Mimesis in, 207 n.; in *Hous of Fame*, 213; mentioned, 29, 50, 75, 178, 201

Horace, 149, 195

Horman's *Vulgaria*, 124

Hosius or Osius, 49

Humours, 169–74

Huon of Bordeaux, 130, 206

Iamblichus, 48

Ibsen, 191

Imitation, the, 18

influences, *v*. Air and Planets

Infortuna Major, 105

Infortuna Minor, 106

Intelligence, distinct from Reason, 88–9, 157

Intelligences, 115–16, 119

internalisation, 42, 203–4, 214–15

Isabel and the Elf-Knight, 124

Isidore, 90–1; on astronomy, 97; on beasts, 148–50; on history, 184, 187

James I (of Scotland), 94, 199

James I (of England), 137–8

Jean de Meung, on Nature, 35, 81; grades of being, 153; mentioned, 18, 59, 75, 114

Jerusalem, 144

Joachim de Flora, 176

Job, 148

John, *v*. Scotus

John, St, 114

Johnson, F. R., 4 n.

Johnson, Dr, his Happy Valley, 145; on *reason*, 158–9, 161; *intellects*, 169; mentioned, 76

Joinville, 177

Josephus, 212, 213

Joshua, 181

Judas Maccabaeus, 181

Julia, 30

Julian the Apostate, 45, 47

Julius Caesar, 181

Jung, 59

Justin Martyr, 49

Juvenal, 149

Kant, 221

Karakorum, 145

Keats, 105, 175, 205, 221

Kempe, Margery, 143

Ker, W. P., 177

Khan, the Great, 145

King, Edward, 213

King Estmere, 187

King of Hearts, 191

Kircher, Athanasius, 124–5, 151

Kirk, Robert, 133, 135

Krapp, G. P., 150 n.

Kublai, 145

Lactantius, 150

Lamb, use of *intellectuals*, 169

lamia, as trans. of *elf*, 124–5

Landor, 80

Langland, on lunacy, 109; planets, 110; on *vis imaginativa*, 163; *donet*, 188

Latham, M. W., 124 n., 137 n.

Latimer, 187

Latino, 187

Launfal, Sir, 130, 131, 132–3

Laȝamon, on daemons, 1–2, 117; mimesis in, 206; mentioned, 209, 211, 212

Lecky, 140

leden, 186

Leibniz, 221

Lilith, 125

Longaevi, the, 122–38

Lovejoy, A. O., 44 n., 97 n., 220 n.

Lucan, 29–34; on the Unnamed, 39; mentioned, 111, 149

Lucretius, 85 n.

Index

Index

Index

Index